Bearmaking 101

An Ins"bear"ational Course

Bearmaking 101

An
Ins"bear"ational
Course

Carol-Lynn Rössel Waugh

Sterling Publishing Co., Inc.
New York

For Nicholas Carl Jonathan Azarian (and Maria Björn)

Acknowledgments

Special thanks to my far-flung "hug" of wonderful, supportive friends who egged, nagged and abetted this tome: Barb Ashleigh Lawrence in New Jersey, Alice Strait in Maine, and Carina Swensson in Sweden. And to Gwyneth Ashcroft in England, who has believed in Maria since she (Maria) was "born." Thanks also to Astrid Engstrand-Holmer and Lill Nylén of Husqvarna Viking, Sweden, who met Nicholas and Maria on their first genealogical journey and sent "stuff" to help their bearmaking project. And to my most patient editor, Isabel Stein, who asked the right questions of this right-brained writer to make this book comprehensible.

Book design by Rose Sheifer
Author's photo on page 2 by PhotoFinish, Augusta, Maine

Library of Congress Cataloging-in-Publication Data Available

10 9 8 7 6 5 4 3 2 1

Published by Sterling Publishing Company, Inc.
387 Park Avenue South, New York, N.Y. 10016

© 1999 by Carol-Lynn Rössel Waugh

Distributed in Canada by Sterling Publishing
c/o Canadian Manda Group, One Atlantic Avenue, Suite 105
Toronto, Ontario, Canada M6K 3E7

Distributed in Great Britain and Europe by Cassell PLC
Wellington House, 125 Strand, London WC2R 0BB, England

Distributed in Australia by Capricorn Link (Australia) Pty Ltd.
P.O. Box 6651, Baulkham Hills, Business Centre, NSW 2153, Australia

Printed in the United States
All rights reserved

Sterling ISBN 0-8069-1373-8

CONTENTS

Materials, Tools, Techniques, and Tips

SECTION I: Fabrics Through Stitching

SECTION II: Jointing and Stuffing

SECTION III: Making Faces

A Björn Teddy Bear Family Album

Introduction

This is not an ordinary bearmaking book. It is a passport and invitation to visit an alternate world, one in which teddy bears pass through dimensional barriers between ordinary reality and imagination to take up residence in the hearts and minds of unsuspecting humans.

The teddies you will meet (and whom you are invited to recreate) are members of a vast clan inhabiting not only the state of Maine but England, Sweden, Russia and many other countries, alongside human companions. Many of the clan, or their ancestors, passed through dimensional gates between the worlds of bears and men, and comfortably inhabit the world humans consider real. As you get to know them, your concept of reality may begin to alter until you, too, will become hard pressed to separate stodgy human fact from fantasy. This is the fervent hope of everyone concerned with this volume.

Bearmaking 101 is a beginning bearmaking book. I chose the simplest methods I know and most readily available materials to present my methods of making bears in a visually oriented, step-by-step method. If you follow the projects in order, you will learn skills which will build upon each other as you create some charming companions. By the end of the book, you should feel pretty competent about your bearmaking abilities.

The methods and patterns used in this book work well for me. They do not pretend to be traditional or to follow anyone else's bearmaking ideas. They certainly are not the only way to make a bear.

If you are a beginner, read the Materials, Tips, and Techniques sections in the second half of the book before starting a project. If you are an advanced bearmaker, most likely you have your own favorite ways of making bears. Feel free to construct the patterns for your own personal use by any method you prefer. These bears aren't fussy about birthing procedures. They just want to enter your life, your home, and your heart.

Note: Most of the bears in this book can be made either with or without humps on their backs. While most modern bears have straightish backs (perhaps because they have learned proper posture), antique, original teddies proudly sported stylish, curvy humps at the top of their backs, like those on real bears. The patterns for jointed bears offer a choice of body patterns: with or without the hump. Enjoy your adventure in bearmaking!

Preamble

Once upon a dream, on a certain Midsummer's Eve, a family of stalwart, artistic, intelligent teddy bears spied the fugitive, flickering light at the edge of their Great Northern Forest, where one of their clan, who happened to be a Wizard, declared the gate to the Other Dimension would open to Seekers with True Sight. They watched: the light shimmered, then almost imperceptibly began changing, sharpening, flickering. The first tendrils of azure-tinged sunlight cut through the fog and, in the fluttering of an eyelid, brushed over the elusive portal. The family of bears joined paws and chased across the fields, just managing to slip between the piney gates to the World of Man before they clicked shut for another season.

This particular gate led to the Central Lakes Region of the great State of Maine, and, as it was not unlike the territory whence they came, the bears set up housekeeping and flourished incongruously in a world of humans and dolls, perhaps because this particular corner of man's reality has for its mascot the Maine black bear. One branch of the family took up residence in a particularly breathtaking spot called BlueBeary Hill, named for an earlier teddish traveler who had a century before passed through the self-same gate. His name was BluBear Yu, and the tale of his great love for Rosa BonneBear, who started a little seminary for lady bears, which became the celebrated Teddy Bear University, is told around campfires by teddies on both sides of the Dimensional Gate.

As our book opens, on a lazy summer afternoon, Maria and Nicholas Björn, the twin younger children of Professor Theodore Roosevelt Björn and his wife Carrie-Lynn, are prowling around the attic of their house on the campus of Teddy Bear University.

Pour yourself a cup of piping, aromatic tea, settle into a favorite comfy chair, and join them as they, and you, discover the adventures to be found between the covers of a rare, old book with the title Bearmaking 101.

For the genealogically inclined, a family album of our bear family is included at the back of this book.

Maria sews a seam

One day last spring, I'd gone to the campus of Teddy Bear University, up on BlueBeary Hill, not far from my home in Winthrop, Maine, to consult with Professor Theodore Roosevelt Björn about the book I was working on ... this book, which came to be called Bearmaking 101.

It was one of those magical days when the misty fog eats up the landscape and makes one imagine she's at the borders of another dimension. And as I chugged up Route 17 towards BlueBeary Hill, the only readily identifiable landmark was the golden dome of BonneBear Hall, the oldest building on campus.

I parked the car and hiked across campus to Professor Ted's big Victorian house, climbed the steps to the wide porch, and rang the bell. Two semi-identical, diamond-shaped brownish noses pressed against the windowpane. I heard a chair crash, a footlike scramble, and the cree-eak of a huge oaken double door as it strained its brass hinges to open.

When it did, two nearly identical little bears were elbowing each other to be first to ask who I was. "You're the writer," said the girl bear. "I'm Maria, of course. And this is Nicholas, but that's not important. I'll take you up because Daddy's waiting already. Although, really, you ought to be asking me about this book. I taught him everything he knows about making bears."

We started climbing the winding oaken staircase.

"So," I said, "how is it you became such an expert in this arcane art, and at such a young age?"

"It was because of the theater," Nick said. "That day we were in the attic looking for trim to put on Goldie's costumes for summer repertory. Mom was pawing through the trunks because it was almost time for Goldie to come up from New York for the season ... and she needed something magical for the duds for ... what was it ... Titania?"

"Goldie's our godmother, you know," Maria said. "Not everyone has a famous actress for a godmother ... Rosalind Golden, Star of Stage and Screen!"

"This trunk, see," Nicholas said, "had all sorts of great stuff in it ... lace and feathers and gewgaws and fabrics you wouldn't believe. But none was magical enough ... and Mom knows about magic, being her father's a wizard ... so we decided to help."

"That's when I found the book ..."

"You might have found it, but I translated it...."

"Right ... after Dad finished the hard part."

"The hard part was working out the designs. And that's why Dad asked you to come. He thought you might want to fix them so human beans could use the plans."

"That's 'beings,'" I said. "I'm eager to ask your father all about it."

"But we can give you a demo."

"And then you can put us in your book."

Maria's embroidered smile was irresistible. I sighed, shook my head, and followed her down the hallway.

"I'll tell Dad you're here!" Nicholas called, as Maria pulled me into the sewing room.

"I hope you have your camera," Maria said, as she fluffed her coiffure and retied her hair ribbon. "I'm wearing my best dress. I ironed it especially for the photo shoot. We start at the beginning: A bear made with only one pattern piece."

Basic Bean Bear

Our first project, Basic Bean Bear (a.k.a. Bear), uses only one pattern piece, yet it will teach you to make a center-seamed head with attached ears: basic skills you will need to make "advanced" bears like Nicholas and Maria.

We will be making bear from a woven-backed mohair fabric. He also looks nifty in woven-backed synthetic fabric: rather fluffy, in fact. If your fabric has a knitted backing, you will need to stabilize it with a lightweight interfacing to prevent it from stretching out of shape and looking peculiar. The new iron-on tricot interfacing or a nonwoven interfacing like Pellon® works well.

Basic Bean Bear is easy to make, comforting in times of trouble and, because of his handy pillowlike physique, a good traveling companion. If you are making him for a child, make him safe by embroidering his eyes with circles of 7/8" (2.2 cm) diameter, the size of a U.S. nickel, with black perle cotton, using satin stitch, as described for the nose. Please read all instructions before cutting pattern or fabric.

Maria and Nicholas at work

- 1/2" yard (.46 m) woven-backed mohair fabric or knitted fabric, which will probably make you two Basic Bean Bears, or one Basic Bean Bear and one Baby Bean Bear, Project 2
- For knitted fabric, iron-on tricot interfacing or nonwoven interfacing
- Two 15 mm glass teddy bear eyes
- Sewing thread to match fabric
- Strong thread (like upholstery thread) to insert eyes and finish
- Long toymaker's (or upholstery) needle
- Sewing machine or hand-sewing needles and thimble
- Permanent fine-line marker
- Sewing shears and embroidery scissors
- Polyester fiberfill
- Plastic dollmaking pellets
- Stuffing stick (e.g., dowel sharpened in pencil sharpener, chopstick, screw driver)
- Small piece of felt or ultrasuede for nose
- Perle embroidery cotton and embroidery needles

Photo 1

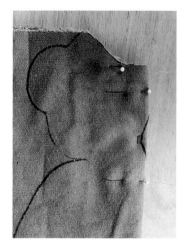

Photo 2

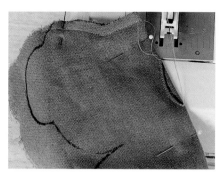

Photo 3

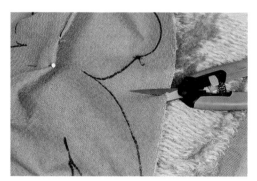

Photo 4

Photo 5

Photo 6

INSTRUCTIONS

Pattern preparation: Photocopy 2-piece pattern at 111% or trace pattern pieces from book and tape the pieces together at joining line. (It could be used at size in book.) Transfer pattern to cardboard or trace onto lightweight rolled plastic to make pattern template. Cut out template shape from cardboard or plastic.

1 First we work on front of bear. Arrange pattern template on back (wrong side) of one layer of fabric, with pile running down body (see Fabric section on mohair for details). Leave enough fabric for another piece the same size as front. Trace around pattern piece with permanent marker.

2 Bear should look something like Photo 1. (Note: photos were taken with an earlier version of bear, so they won't look exactly like pattern.) The pattern's drawn only on one end of the fabric, with ample room for a second piece.

3 With right side of fabric facing down, cut along the top of bear's head from A to C and A´ to C.

4 With right side of fabric folded inside, pin bear's head front together from the forehead (C) to below the neck dart (F). Match A with A´ and B with B´ (Photo 2).

5 Sew seam $1/4$" (.6 cm) inside line, from C to A (Photo 3).

6 Sew neck dart $1/8$" (.3 cm) out from marked curve (Photo 3).

7 Clip each side of fabric to the neck stitch line at E and G, so bear will lie flat (Photo 4).

8 Pin traced bear (front of bear) onto the second large piece of fabric with right sides of fabric facing, making sure the fabric's pile runs down the body on the second piece also. Photo 5 shows the front of the bear pinned to the

bottom layer of fabric, with right sides facing.

9 Without cutting out anything else, sew the two layers together all around bear, $1/8$" (.3 cm) inside drawn line. Be especially careful when sewing close to the clipped edges at E and G.

10 Sew darts at bear's foot creases, on front layer of fabric only, by folding at ankle on each side (Photo 6).

11 Cut out bear on solid line through both layers of fabric.

12 Clip seam allowances at curved edges to seam line, to aid turning, being careful not to cut stitch line.

Photo 7

Photo 8

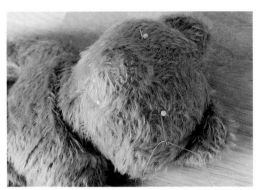

Photo 9

Photo 10

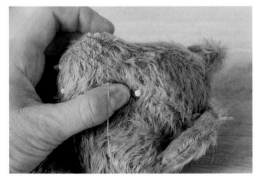

Photo 11

Photo 12

13 Trim away fabric at neck dart (Photo 7).

14 Turn bear over to back. Cut a slit in bear's back for stuffing (Photo 8).

15 Turn bear right-side out. Sew each ear along ear stitch line, starting from outer edge of one ear, across top of head, and down stitch line of other ear.

16 Stuff legs and arms halfway up with polyester fiberfill. (See Stuffing section of Tips and Techniques for details.) Make sure to get the polyester fill nicely down into the ends of the paws. Stuff bear's head firmly with polyester fiberfill. Place bear into a bear-sized container or box and stuff bear's limbs with pellets, leaving lots of room for the pellets to scrunch around.

17 Fill remainder of bear's middle lightly with polyester fiberfill.

18 Sew up the slit in back of bear, still propping him over the container. Use a ladder stitch (see Tips section) and sturdy thread (I use upholstery thread) that matches the mohair to stitch bear closed.

19 Mark location for bear's eyes and mouth with quilter's pins. Thread a long toymaker's (or upholsterer's) needle with sturdy thread. Make a knot at the end of it. Insert it at the pin marking the eye at the (bear's) left side of the head, and bring it out at the pin marking the eye at the right side (Photo 9).

20 Pull the thread up taut on the right side to bring bear's face into shape (Photo 10).

21 Insert needle again into head, near where it exited. Bring it out again at the first pin. Pull up taut again, shaping the head with your hand, and pushing in the area where the eyes will be, to begin to create needle-sculpted eye sockets (Photo 11).

22 Reinsert needle into bear's head at the eye pin and repeat procedure as many times as it takes to needle-sculpt bear's face, gradually pushing out the snout and pushing in the eye sockets (Photo 12).

Photo 13

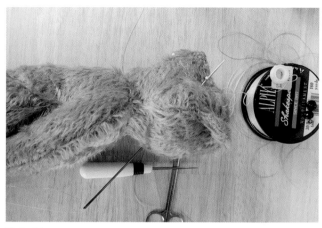

Photo 14

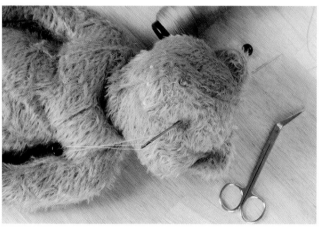

Photo 15

Photo 16

23 Using an awl or the end of sharp embroidery scissors, make a hole at the eye pin on each side of bear's head (Photo 13).

24 Thread sturdy thread onto the long toymaker's needle. Insert it at the back of bear's head and bring it out in front in the hole you've just made at the eye pin (Photo 14).

25 Thread a 15 mm glass teddy bear eye onto the long thread. Insert the needle into the eye hole and bring it out diagonally in back, near the middle of the opposite ear (Photo 15).

26 Situate the eye nicely onto bear's head, fitting the loop on the back of the eye into the hole you've made.

27 Pull the eye thread to the back of bear's head, drawing eye into head (Photo 16).

Photo 17

Photo 18

Photo 19

Photo 20

28 With the thread behind the ear, take a stitch from the back of bear's head into the ear (Photo 17).

29 Bring the needle down again through bear's head and into the metal loop of the eye again. Repeat this procedure until you get the expression you want (Photo 18).

30 Repeat this procedure on the other side of bear's face, making sure to tack down the back of the ear. Nicely shape ear as you do each stitch to the back of the head.

31 Trim bear's nose area to fabric backing. See section of book on Making Faces. You can sew this nose following the freehand style directions for Maria and Nicholas or make a template to cover the nose like the one in Photo 19. If you use a template, trace it onto felt or synthetic suede and cut it out.

32 In Photo 20, bear's nose has been done and framed and we've done the eyebrows. To make them, bring needle with perle cotton from center front of bear's nose upwards. Exit to left of, and above, left eye. Make 45 degree angle stitch above that eye for eyebrow. Bring needle out on opposite side of head, above the right eye. Make stitch above eye at 45 degree angle, completing bear's eyebrows. Exit needle at middle pin indicating location of stitch between nose and mouth. Pull again, sinking eyebrows into head (Photo 20).

Photo 21

Photo 22

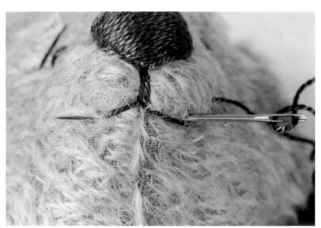
Photo 23

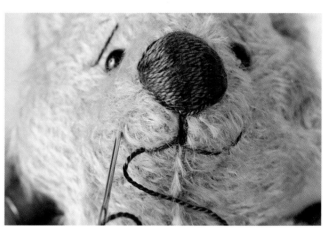
Photo 24

33 Switch to a shorter needle. Stitch upwards towards bear's nose. Exit at pin you inserted at the left side of bear's face that marks the bottom of smile (Photo 21).

34 Insert needle at the center pin again, below bear's nose. Exit at right-side pin (Photo 22). At a 45 degree angle to the straight stitch from nose to mouth, take a stitch upwards. You have completed the inside (bottom) part of bear's smile.

35 To do the outside or framing part of his smile, start from the center below-the-nose point. Take a long stitch underneath the fur, through stuffing, exiting at the pin marking the left end of bear's smile. Bring needle down from this exit point. Take a stitch into the left end of the inside smile. Make the needle skim through stuffing under-neath the inside smile and exit at the right-hand spot where inside smile ends (Photo 23).

36 Repeat procedure above, on right side, to complete upwards swing of right half of smile (Photo 24).

14

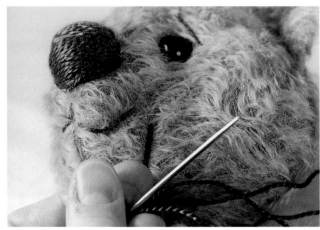

Photo 25

Photo 26

Photo 27

Photo 28

37 Bring needle through to left side of face, slightly below the bottom of bear's smile. Tug on thread to tighten stitch so mouth hugs bear's face (Photo 25).

38 Take a stitch upwards towards nose, at 45 degree angle, slipping needle under mouth stitch to make smile corner of mouth (Photo 26).

39 Stitch through muzzle to opposite side of bear's face. Repeat procedure. Now use a large needle or an awl to fluff out the fur around the face, poking it into bear's head, if necessary, to rearrange the stuffing (needle-sculpting) to your liking.

40 Using long toymaker's needle and thread the color of the fur, take a long, needle-sculpting stitch from neck area under the jaw to upper snout area, to further shape bear's face (Photo 27).

41 Pull the thread taut where it exits to shape facial features (Photo 28).

Photo 29

Photo 30

Photo 31

Photo 32

Photo 33

42 Insert needle from the forehead down through chin, and repeat procedure (steps 40 to 42) as many times as necessary to create the look you want (Photo 29).

43 Using a toothpick to get into difficult spots, glue bear's eyes in place (Photo 30).

44 Using embroidery scissors, trim fur on bear's paw pad area on the bottom half of his arms down to the fabric backing, in a roughly 1" long rectangle. (Feet aren't trimmed yet.)

45 Photo 31 is a closeup showing the trimmed and untrimmed paw pads.

46 Using perle cotton, embroider four long claws onto top (untrimmed part) of paw.

47 Secure claw stitches with a little tacking stitch in the middle of each (Photo 32).

48 Embroider four long claw stitches on each foot, over the end of foot, up to the dart line defining the foot's shape.

49 Secure claw stitches with a little tacking stitch in the middle of each (Photo 33).

50 Trim fur on bottom of each foot down to the fabric backing, as you did for the paw pads.

51 Fluff up bear's hairdo with a metal-toothed comb or brush from the pet shop. Tie a bright bow around bear's neck. Give him a hug, and he's "born"!

Photocopy at 111% and join with Part 2 before cutting fabric.

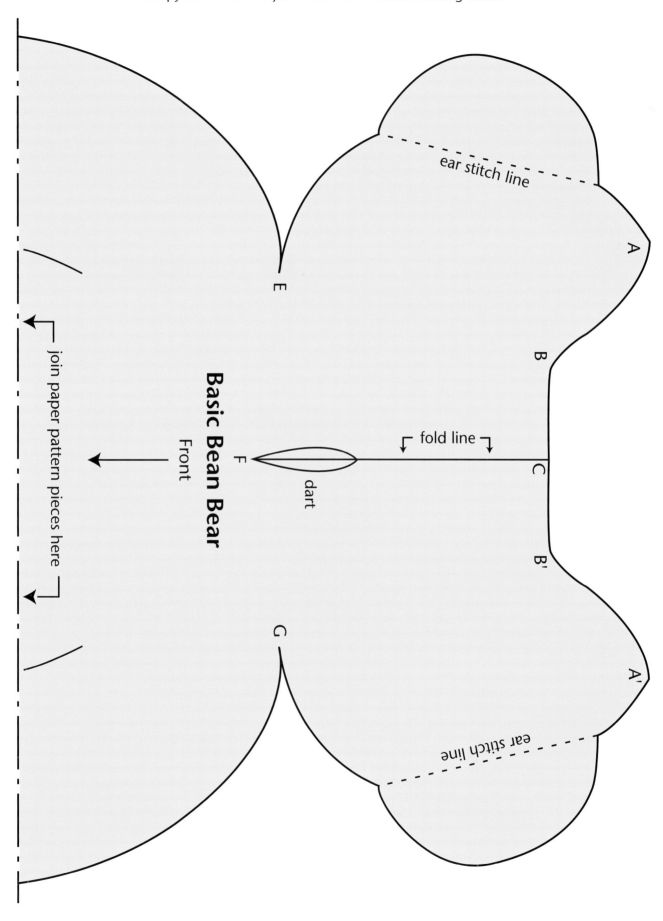

Basic Bean Bear

Front

ear stitch line

A

B

fold line

C

dart

F

E

B'

A'

ear stitch line

G

join paper pattern pieces here

Photocopy at 111% and join with Part 1 before cutting fabric.

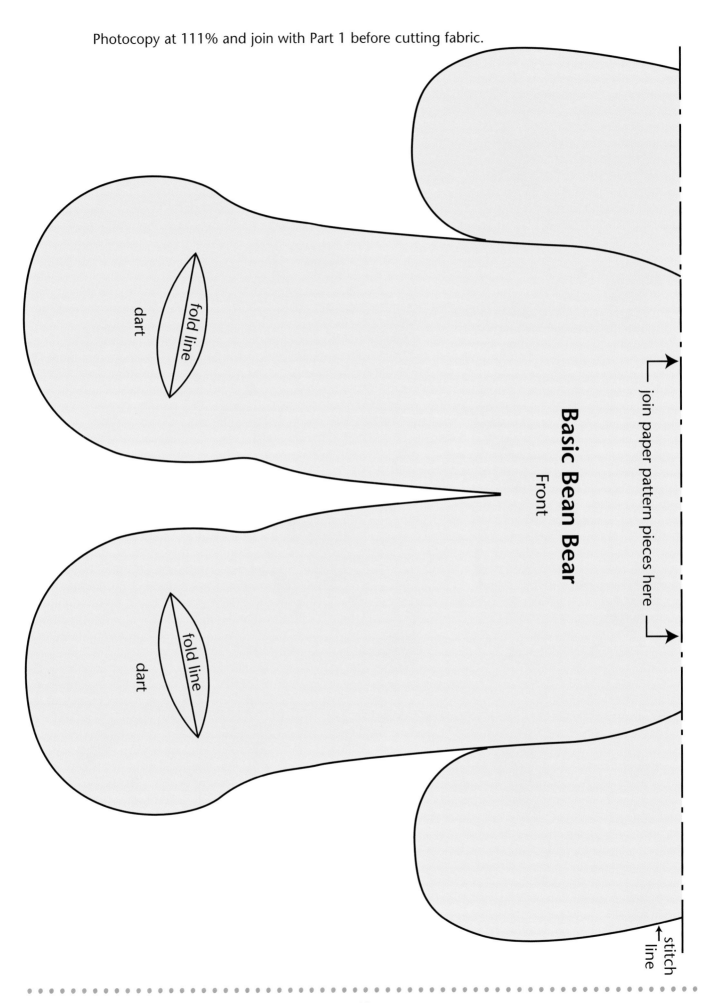

Basic Bean Bear
Front

dart

fold line

dart

fold line

join paper pattern pieces here

stitch
line

18

I got a call the next day from Maria about 7:00 in the morning. Being a nocturnal type, I usually let this type communication go onto the answer machine, but, since the days were nearing their length apex, otherwise known as the summer solstice, I was semi-awake.

The phone voice barked, "I've been up for hours. Where are you? Why is it nobody's ever around to record my great inspirations? And bring donuts!"

Maybe the best donut bakery in Maine lives around the corner from my home on Maranacook Lake, so I bought a bagful and chugged up the hill to the campus. Maria was just about done with the drawing-onto-fabric stages of her second project as I thunked my camera equipment onto the sewing room table.

Baby Bean Bear gets a necklace.

"Nicky said the other bear was too big for him to sleep with," she said, climbing onto the table by the sewing machine. "Sheesh. That bear was a statement. He said he wants a friend."

"Friends are good," I said. "They bring you donuts and hardly ever wake you before dawn.... So this is basically the same as the other bear?"

"Only better! Basic Bean Bear was O.K. This one's my design. More childlike. A Baby Bean Bear. Are you gonna talk or take photos? I wanna get this done before Nicky gets back."

"Sure," I said. "Only if you don't slow down, I get to eat all the donuts."

Baby Bean Bear

- ■ ¼ yard (.23 m) woven-backed mohair fabric
- ■ Two 8 mm or 9 mm shoe buttons or glass teddy bear eyes*
- ■ Sewing thread to match fabric
- ■ Matching strong (upholstery) thread
- ■ Long toymaker's (or upholstery) needle
- ■ Sewing machine or hand-sewing needles
- ■ Embroidery needles
- ■ Thimble. Stuffing stick
- ■ Sewing shears. Embroidery scissors
- ■ Polyester fiberfill
- ■ Plastic dollmaking stuffing pellets
- ■ Permanent fine-line marker
- ■ Small piece felt or synthetic suede
- ■ Perle embroidery cotton for face and claws

If making this bear for a child, please embroider the eyes using black perle cotton.

Our second project, Baby Bean Bear (a.k.a. Baby), uses only one pattern piece, like Basic Bean Bear. Construction techniques are similar, but the bear is closer in size to the next projects you will be tackling. He is made from woven-backed mohair or synthetic fabric.

Maria does some needle-sculpting

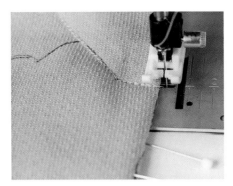

Photo 3

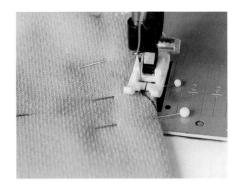

Photo 2

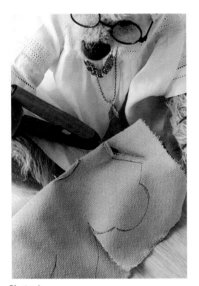

Photo 1

Photo 5

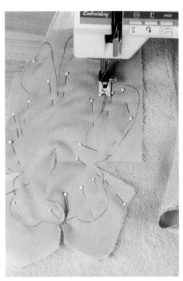

Photo 6

Photo 4

INSTRUCTIONS

Please read all instructions before cutting pattern and fabric, and refer to Tips and Techniques section of book if necessary. Photocopy pattern at 115%.

1 Place your front pattern template onto the wrong side of one thickness of your fabric, arranged so the pile of the fabric runs down the body. Trace around the pattern piece with permanent marker (Photo 1). Leave enough fabric for a second piece the same size.

2 With right side of fabric facing in, fold along center fold line at the top of Baby's head, making sure the edges of

the forehead and the ends of the dart (A and A´) are aligned well. Stitch on the seam line from A to C at the forehead, backstitching at start and finish to reinforce (Photo 2).

3 Sew neck dart exactly on the curved line (Photo 3).

4 Clip each side of fabric rectangle to neck so Baby will lie flat. Trim away fabric leaving a $^{1}/_{8}$" (.3 cm) to $^{1}/_{4}$" (.6 cm) seam allowance outside the line you stitched (Photo 4).

5 Pin front of Baby (right-side down) onto right side of second piece of fabric, making sure the fabric's pile runs downward on body (Photo 5).

6 Sew seam all around Baby, $^{1}/_{16}$" (.15 cm) to $^{1}/_{8}$" (.3 cm) inside drawn line. Be especially careful when sewing close to clipped edges at neck (Photo 6).

Photo 7

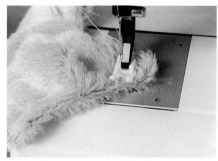

Photo 8

Photo 9

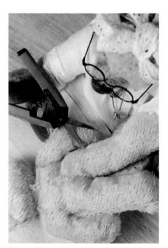

Photo 10

Photo 11

Photo 12

7 The two layers, sewn together, look like Photo 7.

8 Cut out Baby $^{1}/_{4}$" outside stitch line. Clip seam allowances at curved edges of Baby. Clip or trim neck dart.

9 Turn Baby over. Cut a 2" (5 cm) slit in back for stuffing, in torso area.

10 Turn Baby right-side out. Flatten out ears nicely and pin them flat through both layers. Sew each ear along stitch line and from D across top of head and down second ear stitch line, making a continuous stitch line from one ear to other (Photo 8). Reinforce start and finish by back-stitching.

11 Stuff legs and arms halfway with polyester. Make sure to get the poly-ester fill nicely down into the ends of the paws. Stuff Baby's head firmly.

12 Place Baby into a bear-sized con-tainer so pellets don't fly around, and stuff the remainder of Baby with pellets, leaving lots of room for the pellets to

scrunch around. Work lots of pellets into the arms, legs and tummy of Baby, but don't overfill him.

13 Thread strong (upholstery) thread onto needle (Photo 9). Using a ladder stitch (see Closing Seams in Tips and Techniques for reference), sew Baby closed.

14 Trim Baby's paw pad area fur (on the back half of his arms) down to the fabric backing, in a roughly 1" (2.5 cm) long rectangle (Photo 10). Trim bottom of each foot down to fabric backing, as you did for paw pads.

15 Using strong (upholstery) matching thread, sew up Baby's foot darts in front, folding in area indicated on pat-tern piece. This gives him a nice foot (Photo 11).

16 Using strong, matching thread, bring the ends of Baby's ears forward, and sew them in place (Photo 12). This gives the ears more shape.

17 You are now going to shape the bear's face with stitches. This is called needle-sculpting. Thread a dollmaking needle with upholstery thread, knot it at end, and enter the bear's head at the back. Bring the point of the needle out at the spot for the eye on one side (Photo 13). Take a small stitch, and poke the needle again through the head, exiting in back.

18 Now's a good time to determine where you want your bear's features. Mark the location for Baby's mouth with pins. Clip the nose area fur down to the fabric backing. Take a few more stitches: front to back, through the head, each time tugging the thread to sink in the eye area. Do this on both sides of Baby's head for both eyes. (See photos 9 to 12 on page 11.)

Photo 13

Photo 14

Photo 15

Photo 16

Photo 17

Photo 18

Photo 19

Photo 20

19 Using tip of embroidery scissors or an awl, make a small hole where each eye will be, next to the stitch. Thread a longish piece of dental floss or upholstery thread through the eye of a dollmaker's needle; then slip an 8 mm or 9 mm shoe button or glass teddy bear eye onto the thread and knot it. Insert the needle into the hole you've made for the eye, and pull it through, diagonally, to the other side of the head, behind the ear (Photo 14). Tug onto the thread, and settle the eye's loop into the hole. Sew back and forth several times, from back to front, always on the opposite side, catching in the loop underneath the eye each time, and tugging to sink the eye into the eye socket. Repeat on other side of head for second eye.

20 Now for some more needle-sculpting. Thread needle with upholstery thread. Anchor thread at back of Baby's neck and bring out needle at eye level,

catching needle into the loop of one eye (Photo 15).

21 Push the needle through the bridge of the nose, catching the needle in the loop of the other eye, and pull through. Sew back and forth several times. This sinks the eyes into the head and builds up the bridge of the nose. On the last of these stitches, bring needle out through the center of Baby's forehead, just where the bridge of the nose should start. Take a tiny stitch there, and exit under Baby's chin (Photo 16).

22 Make several stitches back and forth, from bridge of nose to throat area, tugging the thread (to needle-sculpt) each time, until you like Baby's snout.

23 See Making Faces section for making nose, mouth, and eyebrows. You can sew this nose following the freehand style directions for Maria or Nicholas, or make a felt template to

cover the nose and stitch over it. Here's a closeup of Baby's face, with features almost done (Photo 17).

24 Using perle cotton, embroider four long claws onto top of paw. Secure claw stitches with a little tacking stitch in the middle of each (Photo 18).

25 Embroider four long claw stitches on each foot and secure with little tacking stitches (Photo 19).

26 Trim Baby's fur around his mouth with embroidery scissors (Photo 20). Dress Baby up with a handmade necklace or a ribbon.

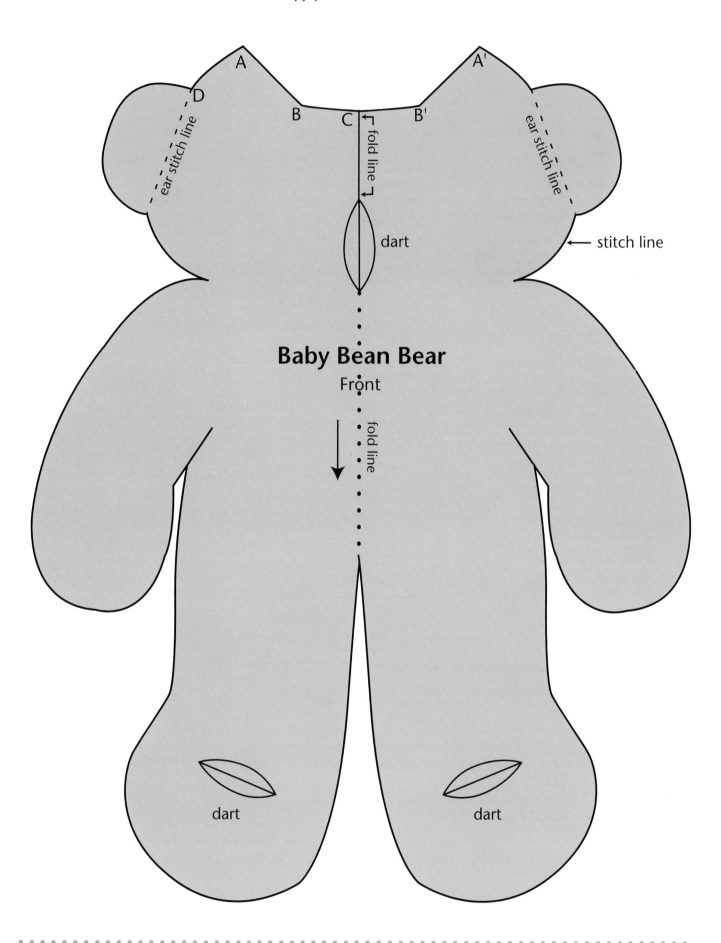

Baby Bean Bear

Front

A gallery of hand puppets, Style 1 and Style 2

"Change of plans!" Maria was dotting a hunk of pink mohair with her set of matrioushka dolls. (Her grand-mother Anastasia is from Arkhangelsk in Northern Russia and the house is full of samovars, Russian shawls, and innumerable matrioushky, or nesting dolls.)

"So, where's Nick?" This was the second session without him. I wondered what the fallout on that would be.

"Over at the theatre. Goldie's here. You know ... Rosalind Golden, Star of Stage and Screen. And she just happens to be our godmother. All three of us, even ole Jenny."

I wondered how pleased Ole Jenny, Maria's grown-up (engaged, even!) sister might be with that comment. I'd spent the afternoon with Jenny-Lynn the day before at the needlework emporium and tea shoppe she and her fiancé, Ed, were trying to get ready before the tourist season was too far advanced.

"Nicky's at the Theatre with Goldie. She says she'll help us put on a puppet show and it can be the summer children's extravaganza. Oboy! So we talked it over with Dad and decided to do a show about the founding of Teddy Bear University ... about how it was a seminary for lady bears in the middle of the 19th century, and Rosa BonneBear and BlåBjörn fell in love and it got to be a University years later when their kids grew up..."

"BlåBjörn?"

"Swedish for 'Blue Bear'. He's some kind of ancestor of ours."

"Ummm." I snapped on the photo lights. "So this is Rosa? Don't you think she's a tad large for you?"

"But not for you. Don't you want to be in the show?"

"I suppose we can show people how to make bears by first doing puppets. They can learn to do heads, and insert eyes, and ... O.K. So, when's this show?"

"Turn on the tape recorder and start focusing. I wanna get Rosa done before Nicky gets back from the theatre."

Rosa BonneBear hand puppet poses with a doll

Teddy Bear Hand Puppet, Style 1

- ¼ yard (.23 m) woven-backed mohair or synthetic pile fabric, pile length ⅜ to ½" (1 to 1.3 cm)
- Small piece of coordinating color cotton velveteen or synthetic suede for paws
- Sewing thread to match fabric
- Dental floss or strong (upholstery) thread for inserting eyes
- Dollmaker's needle. Large-eyed long embroidery needle
- Two 8 mm or 9 mm shoe buttons or teddy bear eyes*
- Perle cotton in coordinating color for features
- Polyester fiberfill
- Sewing machine
- Stuffing stick
- Seam sealant (optional)

If making this puppet for a child, please embroider the eyes using black perle cotton.

Maria cuts out a puppet

Like Maria and Nicholas, I've always loved hand puppets. Part toys, part performers, they come to life in times of solace and celebration. Each time I fit one onto my hand I rediscover the delight and magic of the puppets who shared my fantasies and secret stage plays. And I'm transported back in time, entering a warm, safe realm.

As you make our first puppet project with Maria, you'll use the center-seam head technique you learned in projects 1 and 2. But, this time, the head is shaped through pattern pieces, rather than needle-sculpting. You may notice a family resemblance between our puppets and Maria; it is not entirely by accident. Her comment, when asked, was, "Why make anything but the best?" The bear photographed in this project is Rosa BonneBear. Her features are embroidered with a dark red floss. Her eyes are shoe buttons. Note: this pattern is sized for a medium-sized hand; adjust accordingly before starting if necessary.

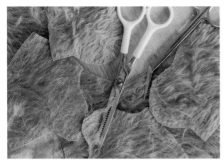

Photo 1

Photo 2

Photo 3

Photo 4

Photo 5

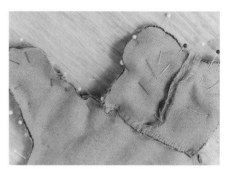

Photo 6

INSTRUCTIONS

Use ¹/₄" (.6 cm) seam allowance throughout. Construction is done with right sides of fabric facing, unless noted.

1   Trace body front and back on folded paper and cut out full patterns from paper. Lay out your pattern pieces on the wrong side of fabric and trace around them with a permanent marker. Be sure the pile of the fabric runs down the body. Cut out pieces along the marker lines, but do not cut out the darts you have marked under the arms yet.

2   Trim the mohair from seam allowances. Give the fur at the two muzzle areas of head front pieces a trimming, making sure you extend the area a bit above the angle in the piece. This is where the eyes will be located (Photo 1).

3   Pin the head front to head front from C to A, and the head back to head back on center back seam line (Photo 2). Pin underarm darts in body front piece (fold the dart, making a crease in the center of the oval you've drawn for the dart).

4   Sew the underarm darts in the body front along the curved lines.

5   Sew the head front pieces together from the edge at A, the bottom of neck, to B, the nose. Clip thread, and then sew from the edge at the top of the head (beyond C) down to nose (B). Clip seam allowances at curves, especially at the juncture between the forehead and the snout.

6   Sew the head back pieces together along center back seam from edge at D to E (bottom to top). Clip seam allowances at curves.

7   Zigzag finish the raw bottom edge of front and back head pieces, finger-pressing seam allowances flat.

8   Pin paw pad to arm from F to G on each side of body front on right side of fabric and sew it on. This paw pad (Photo 3) is made from synthetic suede. Maria is using the Teflon™ foot on this whole project, to make sewing with the "suede" easier. It helps the foot to glide over difficult-to-sew surfaces like suede and leather.

9   Staystitch or zigzag over the bottom edge of each body piece. Machine- or hand-hem the bottom, using a ¹/₄ to ¹/₂" (.6 to 1.3 cm) seam. The puppet pieces, to this step, look like Photo 4.

10   Pin head front and head back to their respective front and back body pieces (Photo 5) and sew; finish edges of seams to keep them from raveling.

11   Pin the front unit to the back unit, finger-pressing neck seam allowances downward (Photo 6). Sew front to back all around.

Photo 7

Photo 8

Photo 9

Photo 10

Photo 11

Photo 12

12 Clip seam allowances of paws and head pieces at curves, especially where they curve around ears.

13 Turn puppet right-side out. Use your stuffing stick to round out ear and nose areas (Photo 7). This is very important. The ears should be nicely rounded. Take your time.

14 Pin the ear areas from I to H, marking the place where ear and head connect. Stitch; begin by sewing back and forth a couple of times at one corner of ear-head juncture. Sew from H to I, across top of head, and from I to H on the other ear, securing this stitching by sewing back and forth a couple of times. Bear puppet should look like Photo 8.

15 Stuff paws about two-thirds of the way, using small bits of fiberfill and rounding the shape of the paw as you stuff. Stuff head the same way, beginning in the nose area, stuffing all around the outer parts of the head to shape it, then filling in the center (Photo 9). Fit the puppet onto your hand, putting thumb and pinky fingers into paws and middle finger into head. Moosh the stuffing around until fingers feel comfortable.

16 About an inch (2.5 cm) from the center front seam, make an eye hole on each side of nose with the sharp tip of embroidery scissors or an awl. Try to do this between the threads of the mohair backing (Photo 10). If this is not possible and you do cut the backing threads, use a drop of seam sealant on the hole and let it dry.

17 Needle-sculpting and eye insertion is best done with strong thread that matches the mohair (upholstery thread is good). If this is not available, dental floss, especially ribbon floss (the flattish kind) works well. Thread a length of thread or floss onto a large-eyed, longish needle. Insert needle into one eye hole. Bring it through head, through bridge of nose area, and out the eye hole on the other side (Photo 11). Tug on the thread, pulling the eye area in closer and pushing the nose area out. Take a few more stitches in the same manner, each time tugging the thread, until you create recessed eye areas to your liking.

Photo 13

Photo 14

Photo 15

18 Test to see that the eye will fit into the hole you've made in head. Enlarge eye hole, if necessary, using seam sealant to keep ends from fraying. Take a stitch with knotted end of dental floss in eye area, then thread eye onto needle. Sew through head, coming out behind ear (Photo 12).

19 Take a small stitch onto ear back, just above the seam you've sewn separating head from ear, coming out at same spot you entered (Photo 13).

20 Insert needle into head and exit at eye, catching your thread into eye loop (Photo 14). Tug thread to set the eye into eye hole. Repeat, each time catching the ear at a different spot, tacking it down in the center. This helps to give the ear a rounded shape. When the eye and ear are to your liking on one side, repeat the technique on the other side of the head.

21 Turn to Making Faces section of book for tips on embroidering your bear puppet's face. See Photo 15 for closeup. Use nose and face directions for center-seamed bear (Nicholas and Maria). See Project 2, step 24 and 25, for embroidering paws (page 23).

Rosa BonneBear is almost ready to play. But first, she needs you to make her true love, BluBear Yu.

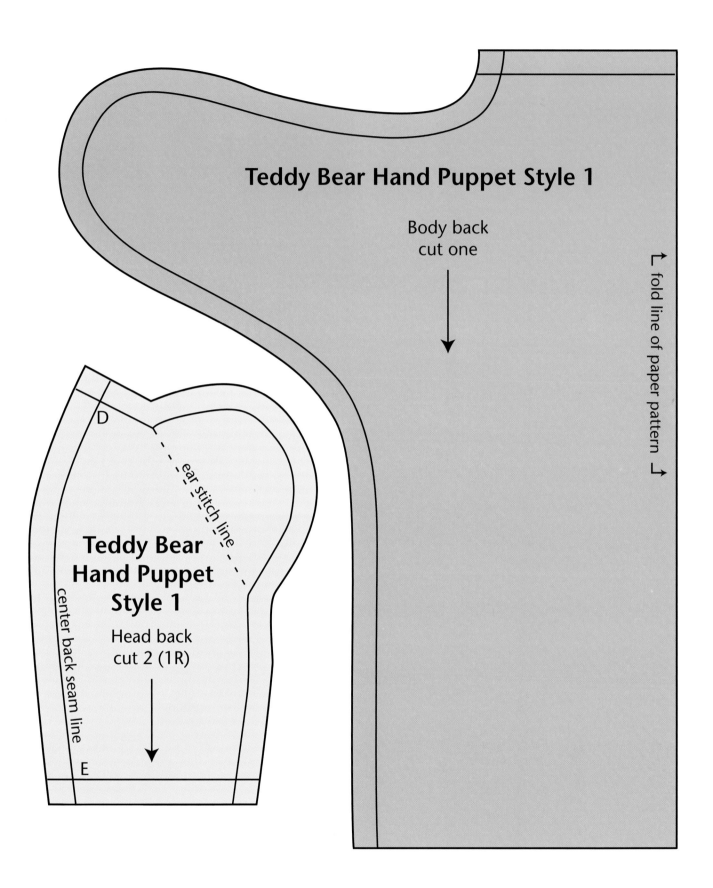

Teddy Bear Hand Puppet Style 1

Body back
cut one

fold line of paper pattern

D

ear stitch line

**Teddy Bear
Hand Puppet
Style 1**

Head back
cut 2 (1R)

center back seam line

E

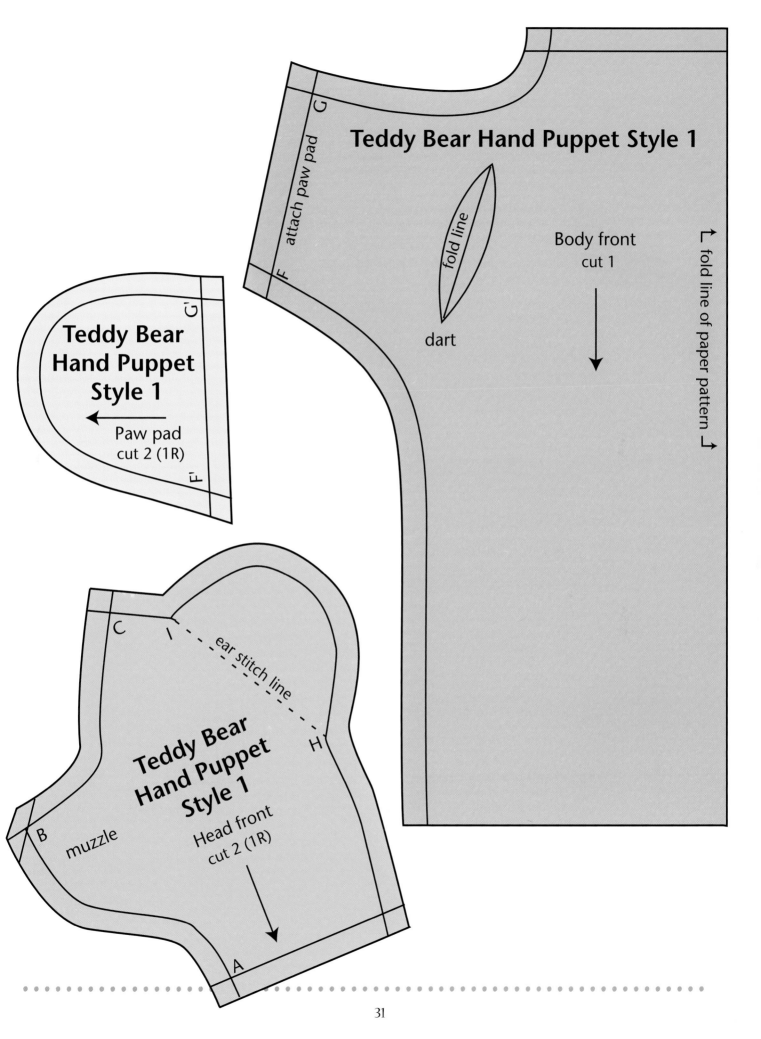

Teddy Bear Hand Puppet Style 1

G

attach paw pad

F

fold line

dart

Body front
cut 1

↑ fold line of paper pattern ↓

**Teddy Bear
Hand Puppet
Style 1**

G'

← Paw pad
cut 2 (1R)

F'

C   I

ear stitch line

H

**Teddy Bear
Hand Puppet
Style 1**

B   muzzle

Head front
cut 2 (1R)

A

"**B**lue is for boys! Also advanced construction techniques." Nicholas spread a huge hunk of dusty blue mohair onto the floor and began drawing pattern pieces onto it with an indelible marker.

"So what's different about this style puppet?" I asked as I snapped on the tape recorder.

"This was the more challenging project in the puppetry book we found in the attic. It's got set-in arms, sorta like on clothing, and the body pieces are different. You get a real front and back. And the head gets set in, not sewn on.

"Also, it's blue. Not exactly the blue of ole BlåBjörn, but Maria didn't see fit to consult me on mohair selection. Now, pay attention as I cut out this guy. I'm gonna need your help. You wanna bring your machine over tomorrow and help me finish them? After all, you're the one who'll be using them."

"Can I keep the ones I make?"

"If anything's left of them at the end of the season."

I snapped on the photo lights and made a note to bring my machine next time. Take a look at the group photo to see how we did. What a bunch of eager bear-type Thespians! Nicholas chose to make his puppet from blue mohair with a ¹/₂" (1.3 cm) long pile. As this lesson opens, you can see he is really getting into his work.

Nicholas cuts some fabric.

Teddy Bear Hand Puppet, Style 2

- ¼ yard (.23 m) woven-backed mohair or synthetic pile fabric, ½" (1.3 cm) long
- Small piece of coordinating color cotton velveteen or synthetic suede (for paws)
- Sewing thread to match fabric
- Dental floss or strong (upholstery) thread for inserting eyes
- Dollmaker's needle. Large-eyed longish embroidery needle
- Two 8 mm or 9 mm shoe buttons or teddy bear eyes*
- Perle cotton in contrasting color for embroidering face and claws
- Polyester fiberfill
- Sewing machine
- Stuffing stick
- Seam sealant (optional)

*If making this puppet for a child, please embroider the eyes using black perle cotton.

Many techniques involved in making the Style 2 puppet are the same as in Style 1. As you perfect them, you will be able to approach making a jointed bear with confidence. The pattern has set-in arms and is a bit more complicated than the Style 1 puppet.

Hand puppets of Maria and Nicholas visit with each other.

Photo 1

Photo 2

Photo 3

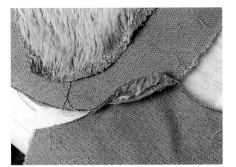

Photo 4

Photo 5

Photo 6

INSTRUCTIONS

Pattern preparation: See Tips and Techniques for pattern preparation. Trace puppet body front and back pattern pieces on folded paper and cut out of paper. Open out pattern to full size to trace on fabric. Trace other pattern pieces onto paper and cut out of paper. Construction is done with right sides of fabric facing and 1/4" (.6 cm) seam allowances throughout, unless noted.

1 On back of fabric, lay out your pattern pieces so pile of fabric runs down body, head and arms. Trace them onto the back side of your mohair with marker. Trace paw pad on paw pad material.

2 Cut out pieces along the marker lines.

3 Trim mohair from seam allowances. Give the two muzzle areas of head front pieces a trimming, making sure you extend to the area a bit above the angle in each piece, where puppet's eyes will be located (Photo 1).

4 With right sides of fabric facing, sew the head front pieces together from the edge of the fabric at A (neck) to B (nose). Clip thread. Sew from the edge of fabric at top of head (C) down to nose (B). Clip seam allowances at curves, especially at the juncture of forehead and snout. Sew the two head back pieces together from the edge at D to E. Clip curves of seam allowances.

5 Zigzag or otherwise finish raw bottom edges of front and back head pieces, finger-pressing seam allowances flat.

6 Finish with zigzag or other stitch bottom edges and neck edges of body pieces and shoulder edges of arms. Stitch front of head to back of head at one side of head only, from bottom edge (F) to G, about halfway up.

7 With strong thread, run a line of gathering stitches at the bottom of the head (neck edge). Or do as in Photo 2, zigzag over a length of dental floss or upholstery thread. When the thread ends are pulled, the neck area will be gathered.

8 Pin front and back halves of head together around the top and down the open side, with right sides of fabric facing. Keeping away from the gathering stitches, sew rest of head together (Photo 3), continuing around head until stitching meets original side seam.

9 Pin front to back body at one shoulder seam, matching X to X´ and Y to Y´, and stitch front to back from X to Y (Photo 4).

10 Stitch a paw pad from I to J on each arm. Finish edges.

11 At top of puppet arm, sew back and forth a couple of times on seam line between M and N (1/2" to either side of center mark O).

12 At O, clip seam allowance to, but not through, stitches.

13 Clip seam allowances at curves on arm and body parts; do not clip deeply, just enough so you can straighten the curves when you pull the piece.

Photo 7

Photo 8

Photo 9

Photo 10

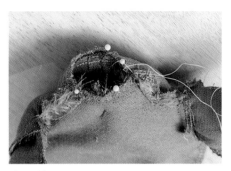

Photo 11

Photo 12

14 Pin, then sew, arm to armhole area of puppet front and back from K to L, right sides together, making sure the sewn-on paw pad points towards the front of puppet's body and O on the arm lines up with the shoulder seam where front and back body meet (Photo 5).

15 Sew second shoulder together as in step 9. Attach second arm as above, Steps 11-14.

16 Pin each side of the body, right sides together, from body bottom (K), around the arm and paw pad (Photo 6). From body bottom on each side, sew up sides, continuing around paw pad (Photo 7). Taper the last portion of your stitches to run into the fold line at the top part of the puppet arm. Reinforce your stitches, and sew off side of arm (Photo 8). Clip paw pad and arm seam allowances at curves.

17 Machine or hand-hem the bottom of the body pieces, using a $^1/4$" to $^1/2$" (.6 to 1.3 cm) hem.

18 The neck areas of the head and body, finished, and the shoulder seams look like Photo 9. Clip seam allowances of head, especially around the ear curves.

19 Turn puppet head right-side out. Use your stuffing tool to round out ear and nose areas. The ears should be nicely rounded.

20 Pin ear areas flat. Begin stitching by backstitching a couple of times on ear seamline starting at H (puppet head is right-side out).

21 Sew along stitch line across ear and across head top to place where other ear connects to head, and stitch other ear stitch line, securing this stitching by backstitching a couple of times. Puppet head should look like Photo 10.

22 Tug on each end of the gathering lines at the neck of puppet head, drawing it in until the opening of the head is slightly smaller than the opening on the puppet body. Tie the gathering threads together, so the head will retain its shape. Insert puppet head into body at the neck with right sides facing. Make

sure the head front is facing the body front. Pin the head to the body (Photo 11). Baste, then machine-sew puppet head to body.

23 Turn puppet right-side out.

24 For stuffing, needle-sculpting, and eye insertion, turn to directions for Puppet 1 (Lesson 3), starting with Step 15. Photo 12 shows puppet with head and paws stuffed.

25 Turn to Making Faces section of book for tips on embroidering your puppet's face and paws. Use directions for center-seamed bears (Nicholas and Maria). Make a freehand or a felt-padded embroidered nose.

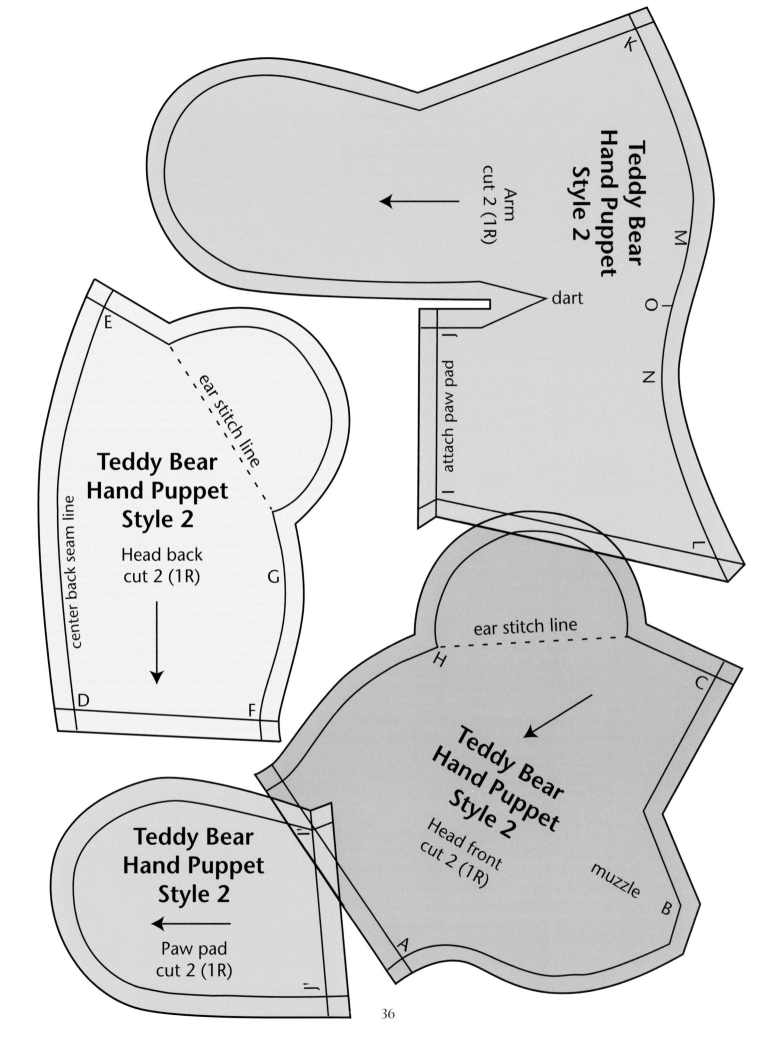

**Teddy Bear
Hand Puppet
Style 2**

Arm
cut 2 (1R)

K

M

O

N

dart

L

J

attach paw pad

I

E

ear stitch line

**Teddy Bear
Hand Puppet
Style 2**

Head back
cut 2 (1R)

center back seam line

G

D

F

ear stitch line

H

C

**Teddy Bear
Hand Puppet
Style 2**

Head front
cut 2 (1R)

muzzle

B

A

**Teddy Bear
Hand Puppet
Style 2**

Paw pad
cut 2 (1R)

J

36

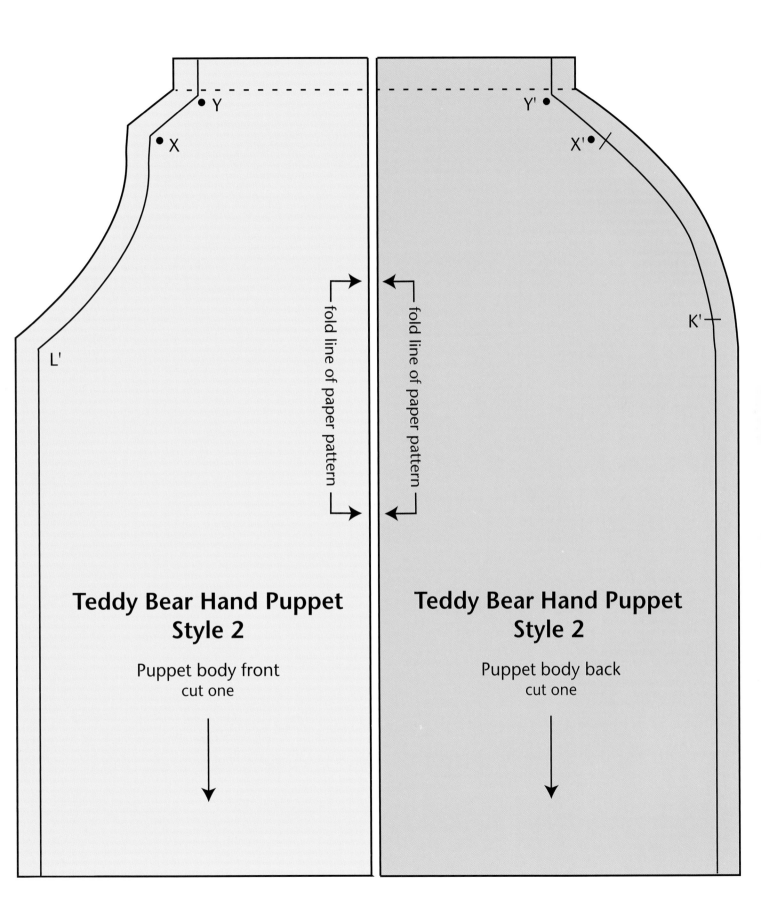

**Teddy Bear Hand Puppet
Style 2**

Puppet body front
cut one

fold line of paper pattern

**Teddy Bear Hand Puppet
Style 2**

Puppet body back
cut one

fold line of paper pattern

Y

X

L'

Y'

X'

K'

“*O*kay, guys; it's time to make jointed bears.*"

Maria threw me an innocent "Who, me?" look. Nick grinned, back-tracked and exited stage left from the sewing room.

"You ever make a jointed bear?"

Maria considered, raised her eyebrows and pursed her lips.

"No time like now," I said. "So, whom do you want to make?"

"Rosa!" Maria grabbed pink mohair leftovers from the hand puppet and ferried them to the table. She was all charm and smiles.

"Tell you what. I'll let you do things you know already, and I'll help with hard parts. It's a good thing I've got auto-focus on this camera."

I discovered that Maria's a good student. She asks questions, undoes and redoes stitching, and wants to master everything right away. Anyway, she wore me out. I didn't leave until maybe 10:00 that night. We'd finished Rosa and cut out a bunch of other bears. Good thing Carrie's got a wonderful samovar in the sewing room. We lived on Russian tea and chopped liver sandwiches, two of my favorites. I wondered if Carrie had frequented the same delis I did in New York. Doing this book, I decided, was getting to be more and more like a visit back home, except with a bearish accent.

This guy has luxurious, thick, curly mohair.

Jointed Teddy Bear with Center-Seam Head

This is my all-time favorite style teddy bear pattern. From it emerged some of my most lovable teddy bear characters: Maria, Nicholas, BluBear Yu, and Rosa BonneBear, who is being "born" in this chapter. There's something honest and simple about a teddy face made without a center gusset to give it shape. This style's nifty for youngish bruins, like Nicholas and Maria. The 11" or 28 cm (small) size is just right for a first try at bearmaking. It's big enough to work on without fiddling, but small enough to take modest space on your shelf but a lot of space in your heart. It won't take a big chunk out of your mohair budget, either.

The 14" or 35.6 cm (large) size is a perfect size for dressing. It's the size of the Maria and Nicholas at work in this book.

This pattern builds upon skills learned making the puppets. Head construction is the same. Paw construction is similar. Large and small bears are made the same way, except for size requirements. Amounts of supplies are listed for both. Choose whichever you like. Note: In addition to a choice of 2 sizes, you have a choice of body types for this bear: with or without hump on back. Before cutting or sewing, please read all instructions.

- Woven-backed sparse mohair or woven-backed synthetic plush: $1/3$ yard (.3 m) for small bear; $1/2$ yard (.46 m) for large one. It may make more than one bear. Pile length: $1/2$" (1.3 cm) for small bear; $5/8$" (1.6 cm) for large bear.

- Square of coordinating or contrasting paw pad fabric: 9" (23 cm) for small bear or 12" (30.5 cm) for large bear

- Two 9 mm (small bear) or 12 mm (large bear) shoe buttons or glass teddy bear eyes*

- Sewing thread or quilting thread to match fabric

- Matching strong thread (like upholstery thread) or dental floss to insert eyes and finish bear

- Long dollmaking or upholstery needle

- Permanent fine-line marker, cardboard, tracing paper

- Sewing machine or hand-sewing needles and thimble

- Sewing shears and embroidery scissors

- For small bear: 10 cotter pins, 1" (2.5 cm) long; 10 small washers (optional). 4 jointing discs for legs, diameter $1^{1}/2$" to $1^{5}/8$" (3.8 to 4 cm). 2 jointing discs for head, diameter $1^{1}/4$" (3.2 cm). 4 jointing discs for arms, diameter 1" (2.5 cm)

  For large bear: 10 cotter pins, $1^{1}/2$" (3.8 cm) long. 10 small washers (optional). 4 jointing discs for legs, diameter 2" (5 cm). 2 jointing discs for head, diameter $1^{1}/2$" (3.8 cm). 4 jointing discs for arms, diameter $1^{1}/2$" (3.8 cm)

- Needle-nose pliers

- Liquid seam sealant

- Polyester fiberfill

- Plastic dollmaking pellets

- Stuffing stick

- Perle embroidery cotton and embroidery needles

- White glue (for eyes)

If this bear is intended for a child, please embroider the eyes and use black perle cotton instead.

Photo 1

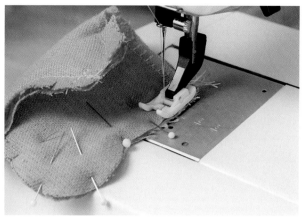

Photo 2

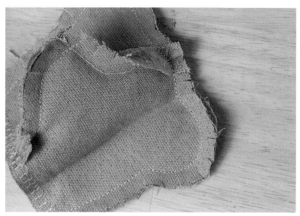

Photo 3

INSTRUCTIONS

Trace any patterns with fold lines onto folded paper and cut out whole shape from paper. Refer to Materials and Tips section of book for preparing patterns, marking fabric and cutting out. Align pattern pieces on wrong side of fabric with pile running down body parts, trace with marker, and cut them out of fabric. Be sure to mark onto the body pattern piece the line indicating where the head is inserted. Construction is done with right sides of fabric facing and 1/4" (.6 cm) seam allowances, unless noted.

1   Trim fur from seam allowances of all pieces. Using embroidery scissors or hair thinning shears (pictured), groom muzzle and area just in back of the corner where nose and forehead join (the eye area). It is easier and neater to clip this area, even tentatively, now, than after the bear is sewn (Photo 1).

2   Sew head front piece from edge at A (neck) to B (nose). Clip sewing thread. Sew from edge at C (top of head) to B (nose). Clip seam allowances at curves, especially at juncture between forehead and snout.

3   Stitch head back pieces together from F to G (bottom to top). Clip seam allowances at curves, without clipping stitches.

4   Finish bottom edge of front and back head pieces, finger-pressing center seam allowances flat. Pin and sew front and back of head together from H, around ears, across, and down other side (Photo 2). Clip seam allowances at curves (Photo 3).

5   Turn head right-side out. Use your stuffing tool to round out ear and nose area. This is very important. You will be creating the ears by sewing across the edges of the ear bumps and they should be nicely rounded. Pin the ear areas flat through both layers, marking spots where ears and head connect. Begin by backstitching a couple of times at one corner of ear-head juncture (J) to reinforce. Sew across ear

stitch line and top of head to place where second ear connects to head; stitch down second ear stitch line, backstitching to secure. Back view of stitching to create ear can be seen in Photo 4.

6   Using sturdy thread or dental floss (best), run a gathering thread along the bottom edge of head by hand or machine.

7   Finish edges of each body piece at stuffing opening with zigzag or other finishing stitch. Pin body pieces together, right sides together. Begin stitching body together before the stuffing opening. Stitch around body and when you come to head insertion point (transferred from pattern), sew back and forth there on seam line until you've reinforced the area. Continue stitching around until you reach the other end of the stuffing opening.

Photo 4

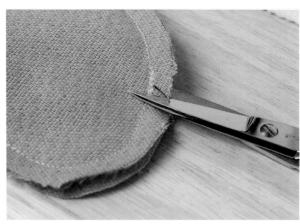

Photo 5

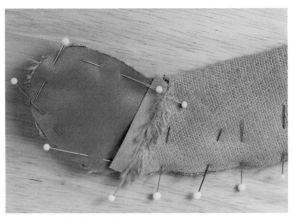

Photo 6

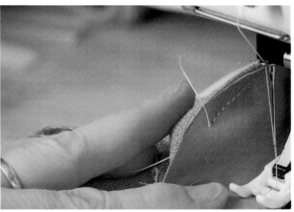

Photo 7

8 Clip seam allowance at head insertion point just into the body fabric (Photo 5). Use liquid seam sealant to prevent fraying. Clip seam allowances at curves around body. Turn body right-side out.

9 Sew paw pads to ends of arms from L to M. If desired, finish top (shoulder) rounded edges of arms with zigzag or other stitch. This helps guide closing stitches and prevents fraying. Do same, if desired, with tops (hips) of legs. Fold each arm along center line and pin (Photo 6). Leaving rounded shoulder of arm open, sew arm from N to L', tapering seam allowance as you come to juncture of paw pad and wrist. Clip curves and turn arms right-side out.

10 Fold legs in half on fold line. Pin. Stitch from bottom to top (R to Q), leaving tops (hip area) open for stuffing.

11 Note: See Tips and Techniques for details of foot pad insertion. Fold foot pad in half the long way. Mark ends of fold with pins. Mark center front and center back of foot with pins. Match together with foot pad pins. Pin foot pads to feet, easing around curves.

12 Stitch pad to foot (Photo 7). If your pads are made of leather or synthetic suede, try using a coated Teflon™ foot like the one pictured. It glides over difficult fabrics easily.

13 Clip seam allowances at curves on legs. Turn legs right-side out.

14 See Tips section of book for stuffing techniques. Stuff paws and feet firmly with fiberfill to ankle or wrist area. Mold and smooth feet and paws (especially) with your hands until they feel good to hold and have no lumps.

Photo 8

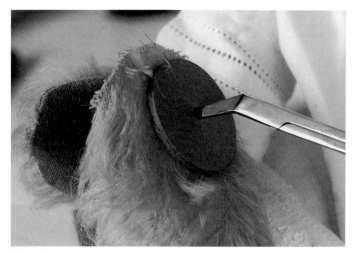
Photo 9

Photo 10

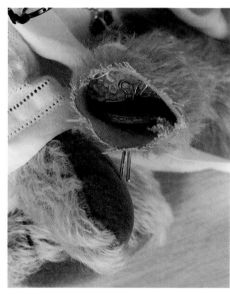
Photo 11

15 Pour plastic doll stuffing pellets into arms and legs, filling area of limb from wrist or ankle to 1" (2.5 cm) above bend in knee or arm. Bend arms as you fill them, to make sure they will move nicely. Leave enough wiggle area at top to fit a disc joint into each limb (Photo 8).

16 Choose a disc for arm or leg to just fit into the limb, with a bit of wiggle room. With limb right-side out, place disc on body side of limb (the side that will face the bear's body), about 3/8" to 1/2" (1 to 1.3 cm) down from top of arm or leg. Use a permanent marker to mark the disc hole. This is where the cotter pin will emerge from arm or leg. Using point of embroidery scissors or awl, make a hole at this point (Photo

9). Try to make this between fibers of fabric. This is not always possible. Use seam sealant to reinforce hole. Let it dry.

17 See the Crown Joints section (p. 110) of the book for instructions on making floppy crown joints. Make one head joint unit and two each of arm and leg joint units. (Sizes of discs are given in Materials list). A "unit" is a disc attached to a cotter pin with a crown joint, plus a second cotter pin (unbent) threaded through the head of the first cotter pin. Insert joint unit in limb and push unbent cotter pin from arm or leg joint through reinforced hole to the right side of the fabric (Photo 10).

18 Top arm or leg with more pellets (Photo 11), then some fiberfill. Use your judgment. The arm joint should move nicely and round nicely at top. The leg joint should also move nicely, but be a tad firmer. The limbs should have a pleasant scrunch to the touch. See p. 116 for how to make ladder stitches, and stitch the tops of limbs closed, using ladder stitch. You may wish to slip a small washer over end of cotter pin on each limb afterwards. This is optional. Some like the way joints feel this way.

Photo 12

Photo 13

Photo 14

Photo 15

19 Stuff head firmly with fiberfill. Insert joint unit into head with unbent cotter pin facing down towards body. Tug on gathering thread at neck to pull neck area closed around cotter pin. You may want to insert a bit more fiberfill to round out head. When head is to your liking, thread a needle onto gathering threads. Sew back and forth over and around cotter pin sticking out bottom of head to close head opening.

20 Your bear should look like Photo 12: four limbs and one head, all stuffed. One empty body.

21 In preparation for face embroidery, mark placement of bear's eyes and mouth (Photo 13). See Making Faces section of book for specifics (p. 119).

22 Needle-sculpt eye area (see Project 1, steps 19 to 30) and thread 9 mm shoe button or glass eye onto sturdy thread or dental floss. Using dollmaker's needle, insert eyes (see Project 1).

23 Embroider face details, then claws on limbs. Here's a closeup of bear's face (Photo 14). See Project 1 for claw details.

24 Lay body, right-side out, on table. Find snip line for head insertion. About 1" (2.5 cm) down from that mark and 1" in from center back, place disc for arm attachment on body. Mark disc hole with permanent marker. This is where arm cotter pin will be attached to body. Place disc for leg attachment at bottom of body, about 3/4" (2 cm) from bottom edge. Mark disc hole with permanent marker. Turn body over. Mark arm and leg disc hole locations on second side the same way (Photo 15).

Photo 16

Photo 18

Photo 17

25   Using awl or embroidery scissors, pierce body at limb insertion marks. Seal edges of holes with seam sealant.

26   Poke cotter pin of head joint through slit at body top into the body cavity. Inside the body, slip another joint disc onto cotter pin (Photo 16) and secure it with a crown joint to hold the head. (See section on making crown joints in Tips part of book.)

27   Making sure arms and legs face the body front, one by one poke the cotter pin of each limb through the appropriate hole in body. Inside body, add a second joint disc to each and secure with a crown joint (Photo 17). Photo 18 shows completed crown joint at arm.

28   Pour a good, scrunchy, supply of doll pellets into bear's tummy and bottom. Fill remainder with polyester fiberfill. Keep bear soft and huggable. Close back seam with ladder stitch.

29   Tie a bow on your bear. Give bear a hug. It's bear's bearthday!

Here's Maria, done in 11" (28 cm) and 15" (38 cm) sizes.

Gallery
of
Bearish Ideas
for Project 5

Change type, color, and length of mohair to create some of Maria's and Nicholas's relations.

If you make the bear of sparse blue mohair, you've recreated BluBear Yu!

Rosa BonneBear in 4 incarnations.

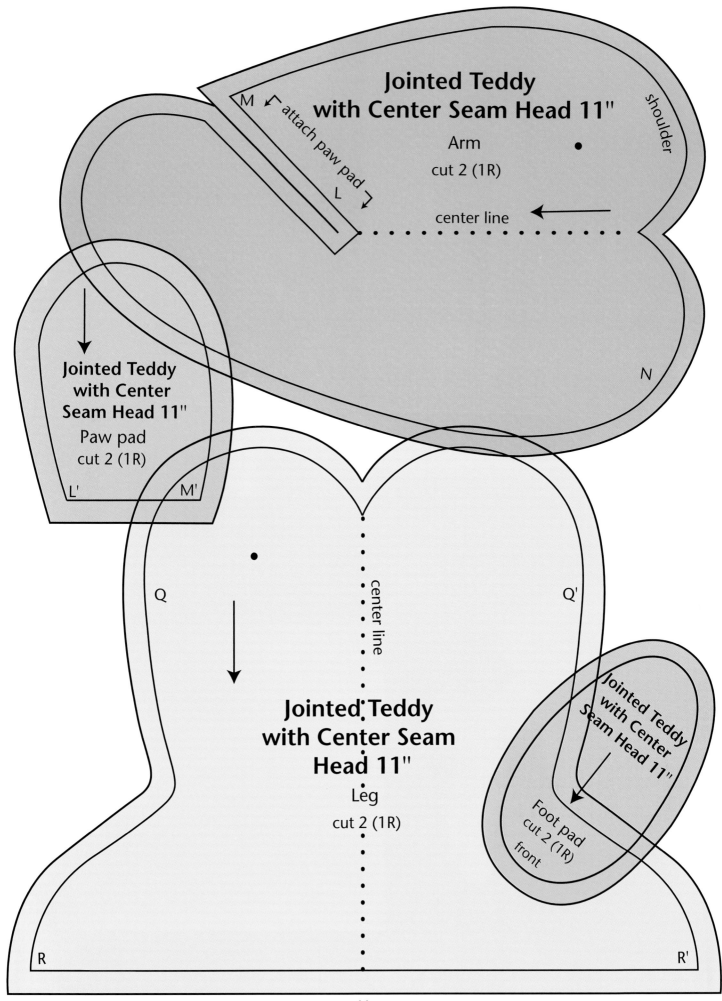

**Jointed Teddy
with Center Seam Head 11"**

Arm

cut 2 (1R)

shoulder

center line

M

attach paw pad

L

N

**Jointed Teddy
with Center
Seam Head 11"**

Paw pad
cut 2 (1R)

L'

M'

Q

center line

Q'

**Jointed Teddy
with Center Seam
Head 11"**

Leg

cut 2 (1R)

**Jointed Teddy
with Center
Seam Head 11"**

Foot pad
cut 2 (1R)
front

R

R'

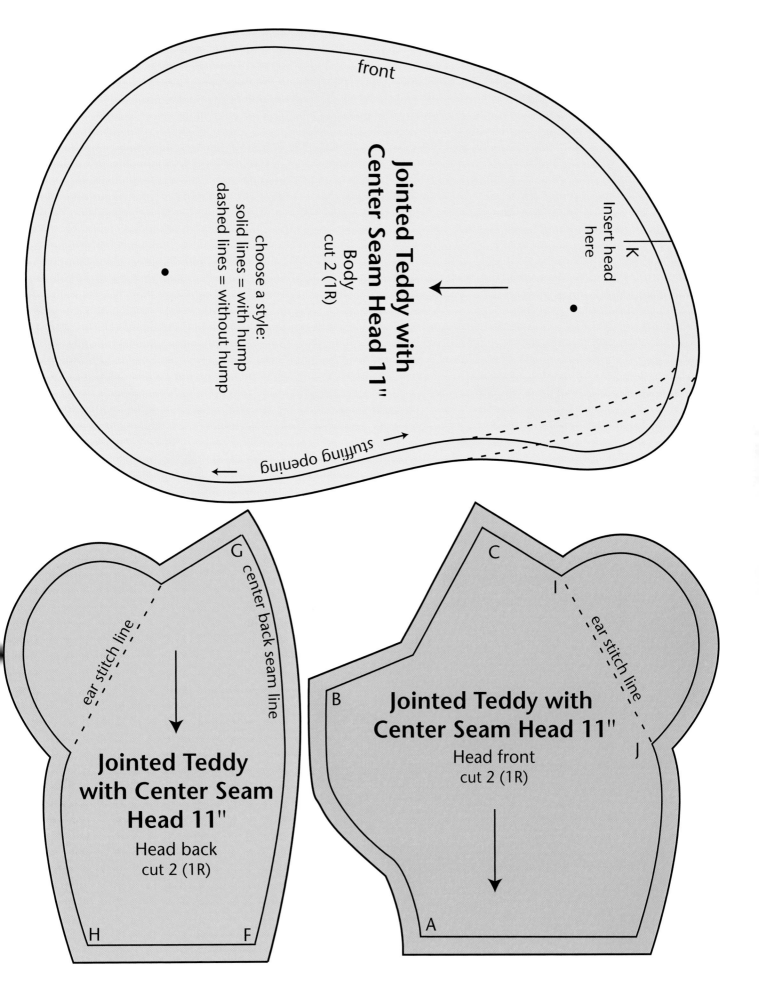

front

Jointed Teddy with
Center Seam Head 11"

Body
cut 2 (1R)

Insert head
here

K

choose a style:
solid lines = with hump
dashed lines = without hump

stuffing opening

G center back seam line

ear stitch line

Jointed Teddy
with Center Seam
Head 11"

Head back
cut 2 (1R)

H   F

C

I

B

Jointed Teddy with
Center Seam Head 11"

Head front
cut 2 (1R)

ear stitch line

J

A

47

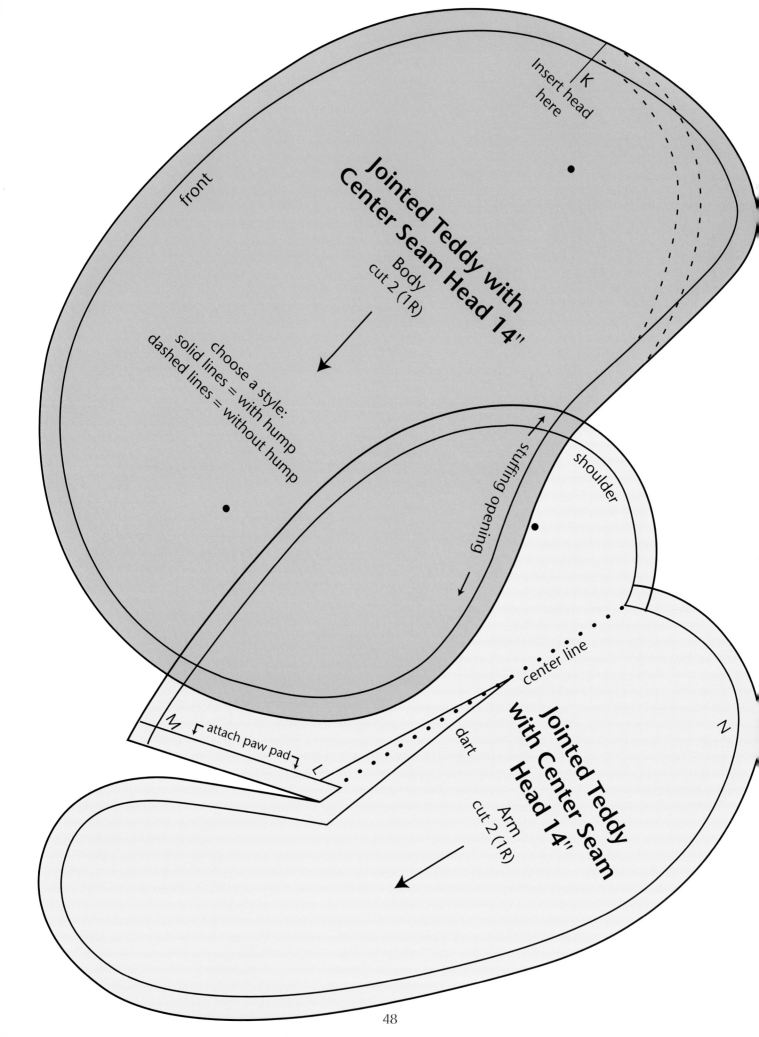

**Jointed Teddy with
Center Seam Head 14"**

Body
cut 2 (1R)

front

Insert head
here

K

choose a style:
solid lines = with hump
dashed lines = without hump

stuffing opening

shoulder

center line

**Jointed Teddy
with Center Seam
Head 14"**

Arm
cut 2 (1R)

dart

N

attach paw pad

M

L

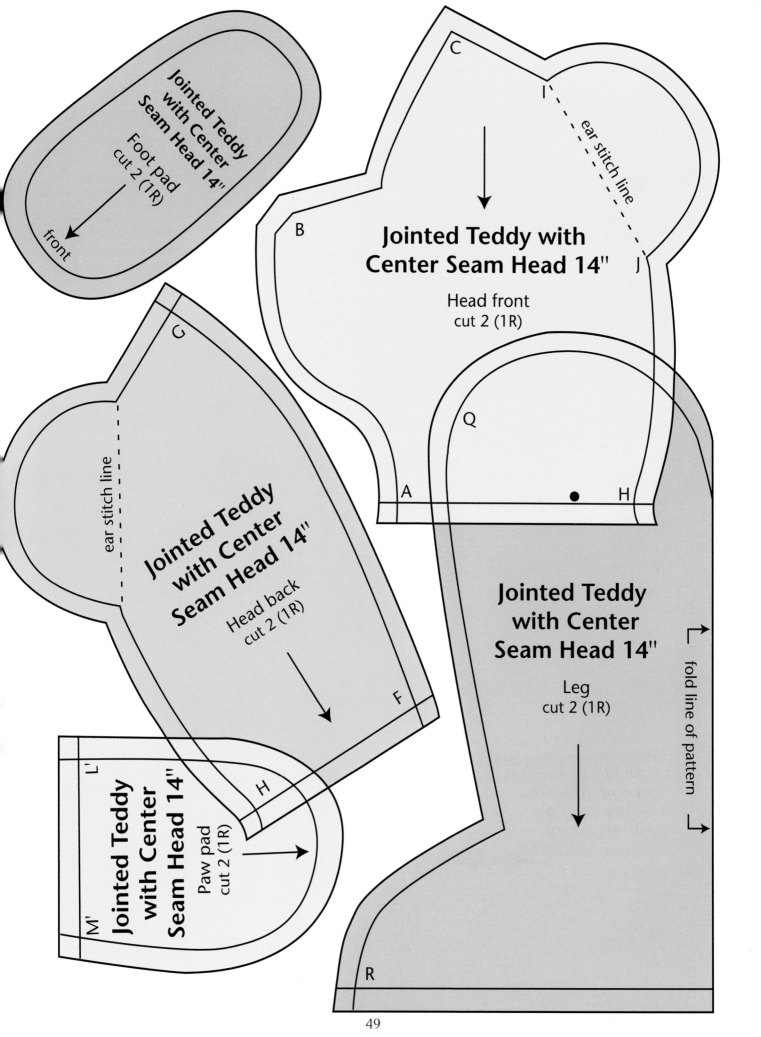

Jointed Teddy
with Center
Seam Head 14"

Foot pad
cut 2 (1R)

front

C

ear stitch line

I'

**Jointed Teddy with
Center Seam Head 14"**

Head front
cut 2 (1R)

B

J'

Q

A

H

G

ear stitch line

*Jointed Teddy
with Center
Seam Head 14"*

Head back
cut 2 (1R)

F

H

L'

**Jointed Teddy with Center
Seam Head 14"**

Paw pad
cut 2 (1R)

M'

**Jointed Teddy
with Center
Seam Head 14"**

Leg
cut 2 (1R)

fold line of pattern

R

Goldie and Maria.

The twins had been busy at least a week making bears with center-seamed heads. I got a chance to do some writing and to go to the theatre and meet Goldie. She said she'd been teaching the godkids to sew and to act since they were little. Goldie had first met Carrie on a photo shoot when Goldie was in high school. She took the train and the ferry and the subway every day from Staten Island into Manhattan to attend the High School of Performing Arts. Goldie needed head shots for a tryout and traded Carrie several months of working as an apprentice for them. When they discovered they'd both grown up on the Island, they became like sisters. Carrie's photos got Goldie her first big paying acting job.

When Carrie moved to Maine to marry Professor Ted, Goldie sorta followed, arranging her schedule so she could act each summer in the Shakespearean Repertory Theatre just down Route 202 from where I live in Winthrop. Carrie does stage and costume design (subjects she teaches at TBU) and is the acting company's publicity photographer. We discovered we had a lot to talk about.

"So what's all this about the puppet show?" I asked.

"Haven't you heard," asked Goldie. "It's expanded into a puppet-cum-marionette experience."

"Whose big idea was that?"

"Need you ask? Maria got the notion to do a bear puppet of her father. Somehow she expanded that idea into its becoming a marionette."

"How's it coming?" I asked.

"They've got a little problem ... something called 'gussets'? Of course, it could have been 'buzzards.' It's hard to understand Maria when she's frustrated."

"I'm off," I said. And I headed back to campus, lest a certain young bear explode.

That afternoon was one of the longer ones of the summer. But after a lot of surprisingly patient taking out and redoing on Maria's part, she learned to "clone" her Dad, in two sizes. The smaller of the two was just right for marionette duty.

Teatime for Carrie.

Jointed Teddy Bear with Gusseted Head

The styling of this bear is more traditional than the one in Project 5. Bear's head features a gusset, a piece added in the center for shaping. Bear has ears that are sewn into the head, not onto it. Bear's body has an antiquey shape with a slight hump in back. Darts at top and bottom give it shape. Because of its proportions, this teddy tends to look older than those of the last project. Bear's limbs are long and shapely, reminiscent of old-time teddies, yet this bear is definitely a modern invention.

You have a choice of two sizes of bear here. I developed the large size of this bear first. I wanted a teddy large enough to wear off-the-rack infant clothing, because my bruins are clothing-conscious. I found sizes of infant clothes vary; it's best to bring the bear with you when you shop. I do.

The smaller of the two sizes is in proportion with the 11" (28 cm) Rosa bear in the previous project. Their body parts may be interchanged with each other, and the limbs replaced with the multijointed limbs in Project 7 to create new combinations and characters. (This won't work with the larger sizes.)

If you wish to make a hand puppet of Professor Ted or Carrie, you can substitute the head of the 11" (28 cm) bear in this project for the center-seamed Rosa head in Project 4. This pattern builds upon skills learned making Project 5. Arm and leg construction are the same. Jointing is similar. 11" and 22" (56 cm) bears are made the same, except for size requirements.

MATERIALS AND SUPPLIES

- Woven-backed sparse mohair or woven-backed synthetic plush: 1/3 yard (.3 m) for small bear; 5/8 yard (.6 m) for large bear. Pile length, 1/2" (1.3 cm) for small bear; 5/8" (1.6 cm) for large bear
- Square of coordinating or contrasting paw pad fabric: 9" (23 cm) for small bear; 12" (30.5 cm) for large bear
- Small piece of felt that matches color of embroidery floss for nose
- Shoe buttons or glass teddy bear eyes: two 9 mm (small bear) or 15 mm (large bear)*
- Sewing thread to match fabric (quilting thread works well)
- Matching strong thread (like upholstery thread) or dental floss to insert eyes and finish bear
- Long dollmaking or upholstery needle
- Permanent fine-line marker
- Cardboard and tracing paper for making pattern
- Sewing machine or hand-sewing needles and thimble
- Sewing shears and embroidery scissors
- For small bear: 10 cotter pins, 1" (2.5 cm) long; 10 small washers (optional). 4 jointing discs for legs, diameter 1 1/2" to 1 5/8" (3.8 to 4 cm). 2 jointing discs for head, diameter 1 1/4" (3.2 cm). 4 jointing discs for arms, diameter 1" (2.5 cm)
  For large bear: 10 cotter pins, 1 1/2" (3.8 cm) long. 10 small washers (optional). 4 jointing discs for legs, diameter 2 1/2 to 2 5/8" (6.4 to 6.7 cm). 2 jointing discs for head, diameter 2" (5.1 cm). 4 jointing discs for arms, diameter 2 1/4 to 2 1/2" (5.7 to 6.4 cm)
- Needle-nose pliers
- Liquid seam sealant
- Polyester fiberfill
- Plastic dollmaking pellets
- Stuffing stick
- Perle embroidery cotton for nose and mouth. Large-eyed embroidery needles
- White glue and toothpick (for eyes)

*If this bear is intended for a child, please embroider the eyes with black perle cotton.

Photo 1

Photo 2

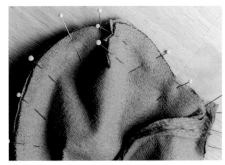
Photo 3

Photo 4

Photo 5

INSTRUCTIONS

Before cutting or sewing, kindly read all instructions. If making large size bear, trace gusset and arm patterns on folded paper and cut out of paper. Work with full patterns on fabric. Align pattern pieces on wrong side of fabric so pile of fabric runs down body, head, and limbs. Refer to Materials and Tips section for preparing pattern, fabric, and cutting out, if necessary. Construction is done with right sides of fabric facing, unless otherwise noted, and $1/4$" .6 cm) seam allowances.

1   Cut out bear body pieces and paws from their respective fabrics. Trim fur from seam allowances of all pieces. Using embroidery scissors or hair thinning shears, thin fur at nose area of gusset from straight edge at front to just past area where it begins to flare out at the sides; this is eye area.

2   If your bear is a girl, trim muzzle area of each head piece, from eye area down to chin (Photo 1).

3   Pin the darts, top and bottom, of each body piece. Pin dart at bottom of each head piece. For each ear, pin 2 ear pieces together (1 and reversed) around top curve from M to N and sew around curve.

4   Take 2 head pieces and pin seam at jaw of bear together from edge at A to

B and sew. Finish edges of sewn seam allowances with zigzag or other finishing stitch. Sew bottom darts on head closed.

5   Finish neck area of the bear's head with zigzag or other stitch, finger-pressing seam allowances flat.

6   Fold nose area of gusset in half longways on center line (fold line of pattern). Pin at center.

7   Finger-press open central seam allowance at bear's jaw.

8   Pin gusset into head so center of nose line (B´) of gusset aligns with head seam line at B. Stitch gusset to head on this nose line, backstitching at each end of seam (Photo 2).

9   Pin dart at top of each side of the bear's head together, temporarily. Pin each side of the bear's head to rest of gusset, gently easing gusset along curves in head (Photo 3). Match the area where the gusset flares out with the area where the forehead flares out. Ease bottom part of gusset so it exactly fits back of head and ends at neck bottom (C).

10   On each side of head, stitch downward from unsewn dart (E) to nose area (B), connecting one side of head with side of gusset. Ease sides of nose area

into seam. Note: $1/4$" (.6 cm) seam allowance of unsewn dart is folded over and taken up into gusset seam.

11   Sew back of head to gusset on each side, from dart at top (F) to bottom of neck (C). Set aside.

12   Clip seam allowances on stitched curves of ears. Turn ears right-side out. Fold about $1/2$" (1.3 cm) of sides of ears to front, pin, stitch in place, and finish seam allowance edge (Photo 4).

13   Cut ear line into each side of gusset at top of head (these abut the 2 unsewn darts at the top of head). Trim seam allowances of the darts you've pinned together at EF at an angle, tapering seam allowance to point of dart. This slit, extending from gusset to include dart opening, is where you will insert an ear.

14   Fold each ear in half. Mark center of ear with a pin. With turned-in side of ear facing front (towards the nose), pin each ear into head, aligning the center ear pin with the head-gusset seam line.

15   Sew ears into head with straight stitch. Finish seam with zigzag or other finishing stitch. Turn head right-side out. The sewn-in ear looks like Photo 5, nice and curvy.

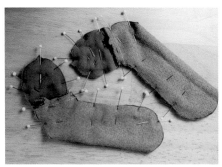

Photo 6

Photo 7

Photo 8

Photo 9

16 Finish top open raw edges of each arm or leg with zigzag or other finishing stitch and finish the stuffing opening raw edges of each body piece also. Each will be hand-sewn closed later on.

17 Pin, then sew, paw pad to each arm from O to P.

18 Fold arm in half, right sides together, on fold line. Pin around paw and up arm, leaving rounded top area (shoulder) open (Photo 6) for stuffing and jointing. Sew arm sides together from top to down all around paw. Taper your seam allowance as you finish sewing the wrist of paw on folded side of arm, so your stitches run into the fold of the arm. Repeat for second arm.

19 Edge-finish (optional) raw bottom edge of each foot. This helps control the shape as you insert the foot pad. Then pin two sides of each leg together, leaving rounded top (hip) open from G to H for stuffing. Sew leg pieces together from J to G (toe to center top) and from I to H (Photo 7). Reinforce stitches at both ends with backstitching.

20 Fold foot pad in half on long axis from front to back. Front is wider than back. Mark center front and center back with pins. Match foot pad center front with center front seam of leg at J.

Match center back of foot pad with center back seam at I and pin pad into foot, easing around curves. Baste if desired and stitch foot pad to foot. Use a pusher stick, such as a barbecue skewer, to guide fabric around curves (and save your fingertips) if you wish when stitching. Finish foot pad seam with zigzag or other finishing stitch.

21 Pin sides of body together, finger-pressing dart seam allowances flat, top and bottom. Sew together, leaving stuffing opening unstitched (Photo 8).

22 With strong thread (upholstery thread or dental floss) in needle, run a line of gathering stitches on head at neck edge.

23 Stuff the bear's limbs as shown in Tips and Techniques section on stuffing.

24 Please refer to Crown Joint section about how to make wobbly (double) cotter pin joints. Make one crown joint on a disc for each arm, each leg, and for the head (see Materials list for disc sizes). Thread an unbent cotter pin through the head of the bent cotter pin for each unit, to make double cotter-pin wobble joints for this bear's limbs. Slip a washer over both legs of each unbent cotter pin.

25 Insert a joint unit into each limb, following directions in Tips and Techniques (p. 113). The unbent cotter pin should be sticking out. After the joint unit is inserted in limb, close opening using strong thread or dental floss and the ladder stitch, leaving the unbent cotter pin sticking out (see Stuffing Tips for reference).

26 Stuff head firmly with fiberfill. After head is mostly stuffed, insert disc the crown joint unit for the head into head's open neck, with its unbent cotter pin facing out. The head should already have a line of gathering stitches run around the neck opening. Gather thread snugly, until no trace of the disc can be seen and the cotter pin dangles down. Stitch back and forth around cotter pin legs, using thread you've pulled taut, until bottom of head is securely closed.

27 Take the bear's head in your hand. Smoosh nose upwards and ears downwards. This is Step 1 for needle-sculpting the bear's face (Photo 9).

28 Cut out the shape you want for the bear's nose from felt, for a template (see Making Faces section of book, page 124). Pin and then tack-stitch template to the bear's face in nose area of gusset. This will guide your needle-sculpting.

Photo 10

Photo 11

Photo 12

Photo 13

29 Thread a dollmaker's or upholstery needle with sturdy thread matching fur. Knot one end with a big, strong knot. Insert needle and bury the knot in seam allowance at point on head where gusset stops being straightish and begins to flare out to form forehead. Exit directly opposite, on other side of snout (Photo 10).

30 Tug hard on thread. You are pulling the sides of the gusset together and up, from underneath, to form eye sockets and a lovely snout (Photo 11). Take a small stitch beside the spot your needle exited. Repeat in opposite direction, exiting where you began. Your bear's face is beginning to take shape. Repeat this process three or four times, until

the eye sockets deepen and the nose rounds to your satisfaction. Exit needle through back of head. Clip thread. Lose thread in plush.

31 Thread a dollmaker's needle with sturdy thread matching fur. Knot one end. Insert needle and bury knot in center seam at bottom of the bear's snout area, where snout meets neck. Sew through snout, exiting at center of gusset, at eye level. Take a little stitch, returning where you started (Photo 12).

32 Tug on thread. The gusset pulls up and in, defining the break between nose and forehead. Continue taking stitches: one on either side of central one, in turn, until gusset/forehead area

is needle-sculpted to your liking. Exit thread through back of head. Clip. Lose thread in plush.

33 Using long dollmaker's or upholsterer's needle and upholstery thread, insert eyes into bear's head. See Project 1 for specifics of how to insert eyes. This can be done before or after embroidering nose. I've done it both ways.

34 Embroider bear's face. See Making Faces section of book for details of nose for gusseted head. Photo 13 is a closeup.

35 Embroider bear's feet and paws with claws, using perle cotton. See Project 1 for reference.

Photo 14

Photo 15

Photo 16

Photo 17

36 If you are making bear into a marionette or if you just want his knees and elbows extra bendable, this is the time to take a few stitches with strong, matching thread through knee and elbow area (Photo 14). Fiddle with stuffing before stitching to get the proper feel for limbs. They should flop nicely.

37 Needle-sculpted arms and legs look like Photo 15.

38 To attach bear's head to body at spot where sections of body come together at top,. make a hole at body top with sharp point (embroidery scissors or awl); body isn't stuffed yet

(Photo 16). Insert head's unbent cotter pin into hole you just pierced. On the inside of body, top cotter pin with a head jointing disc and make a crown joint (See p.110).

39 For limbs, with a sharp point (embroidery scissors or awl) make holes in the body at the dots on pattern just below the top darts for the arms (Photo 17) and just above the bottom darts at hips for the legs. Protect the holes with seam sealant to keep from fraying.

40 With arm facing front of body on each side (paw pad facing body), poke each arm's cotter pin into the correct hole at the bottom of the

shoulder dart, add joint disc inside body, and make a crown joint inside bear's body to hold arm. See p. 44, Photo 18, for reference.

41 Insert leg's cotter pin into leg hole of body, being sure foot faces forward, add joint disc inside body, and make crown joint inside body to hold leg. Do second leg the same way.

42 Glue bear's eyes in place using a toothpick dipped into white glue.

43 Bear's body is ready for stuffing and closing. Please see Stuffing Tips section of book for details. Stitch body closed with ladder stitch after stuffing.

Gallery
of
Professor Teds
and Carries

Here's a large Professor Ted, done with wobble jointing.

Large-size Carrie and Professor Ted bears, made with wobble joints.

Here's the original Professor Ted. He was made with regular cotter pin crown joints, using just one cotter pin per joint. The difference in posture and attitude is because of jointing methods.

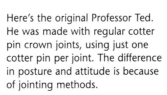

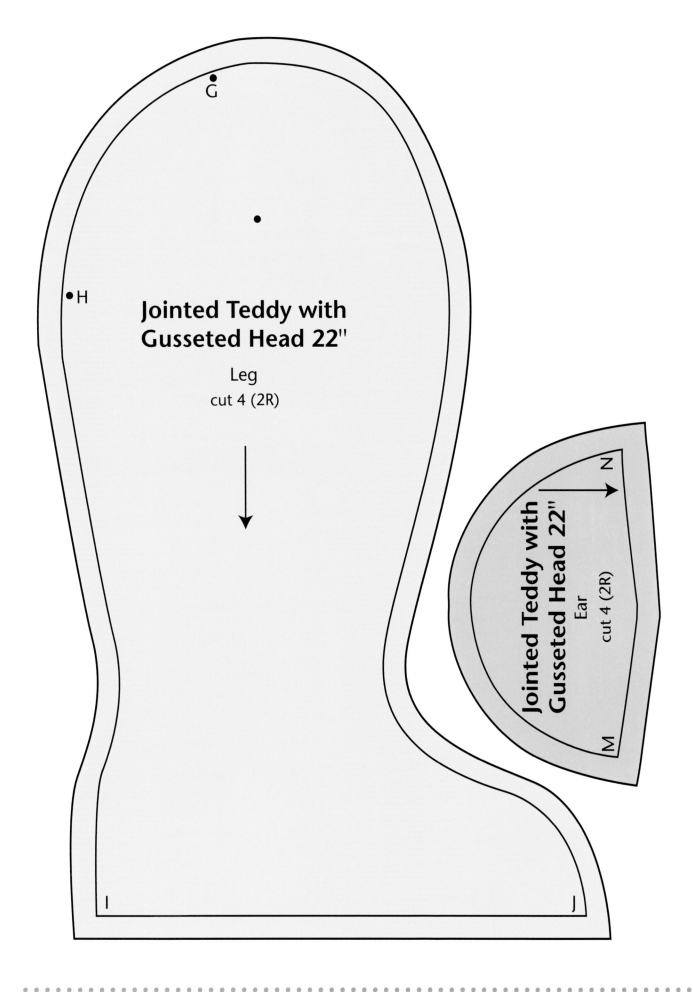

**Jointed Teddy with
Gusseted Head 22"**

Leg
cut 4 (2R)

G

●H

**Jointed Teddy with
Gusseted Head 22"**
Ear
cut 4 (2R)

N

M

I

J

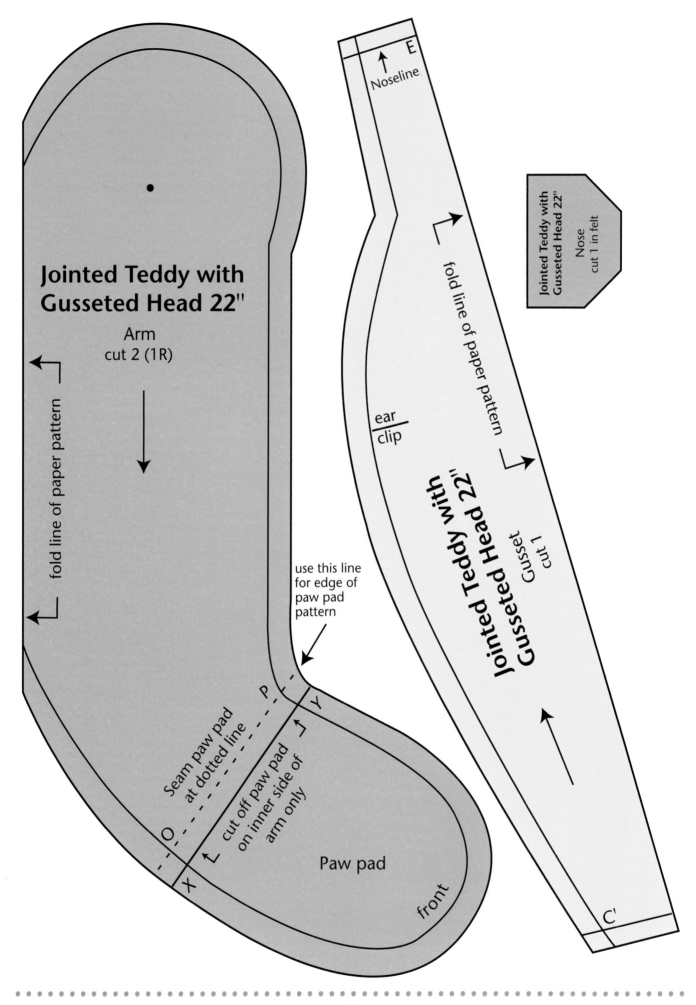

Jointed Teddy with Gusseted Head 22"

Arm
cut 2 (1R)

fold line of paper pattern

use this line for edge of paw pad pattern

Seam paw pad at dotted line

cut off paw pad on inner side of arm only

P

Y

O

X

Paw pad

front

E

Noseline

ear
clip

fold line of paper pattern

Jointed Teddy with Gusseted Head 22"

Gusset
cut 1

C'

Jointed Teddy with Gusseted Head 22"
Nose
cut 1 in felt

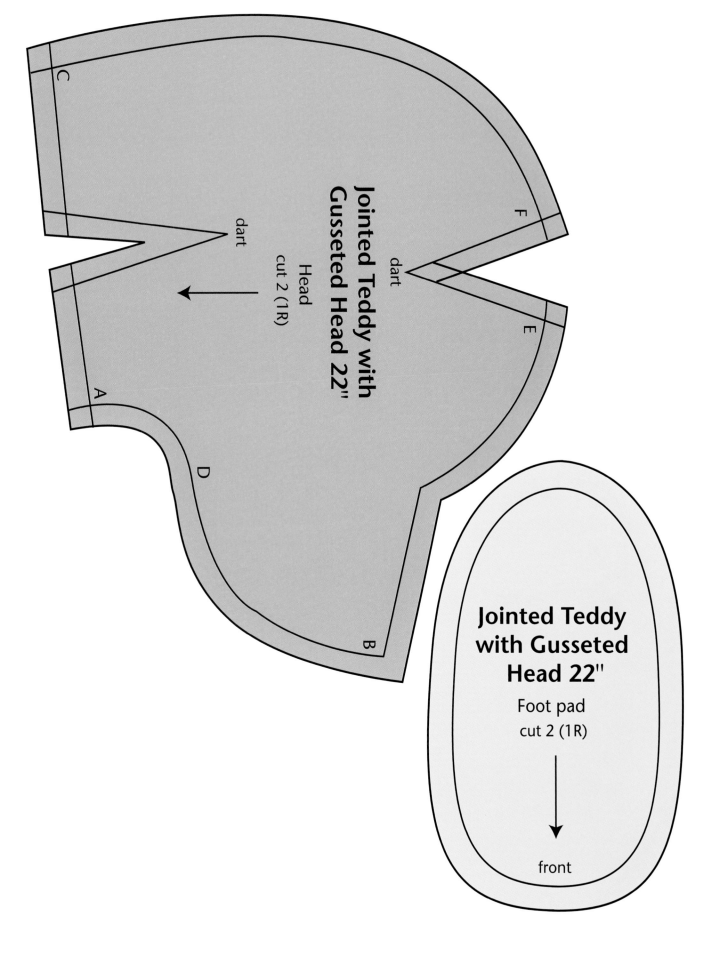

Jointed Teddy with Gusseted Head 22"

Head
cut 2 (1R)

dart

dart

C

F

E

A

D

B

Jointed Teddy with Gusseted Head 22"

Foot pad
cut 2 (1R)

front

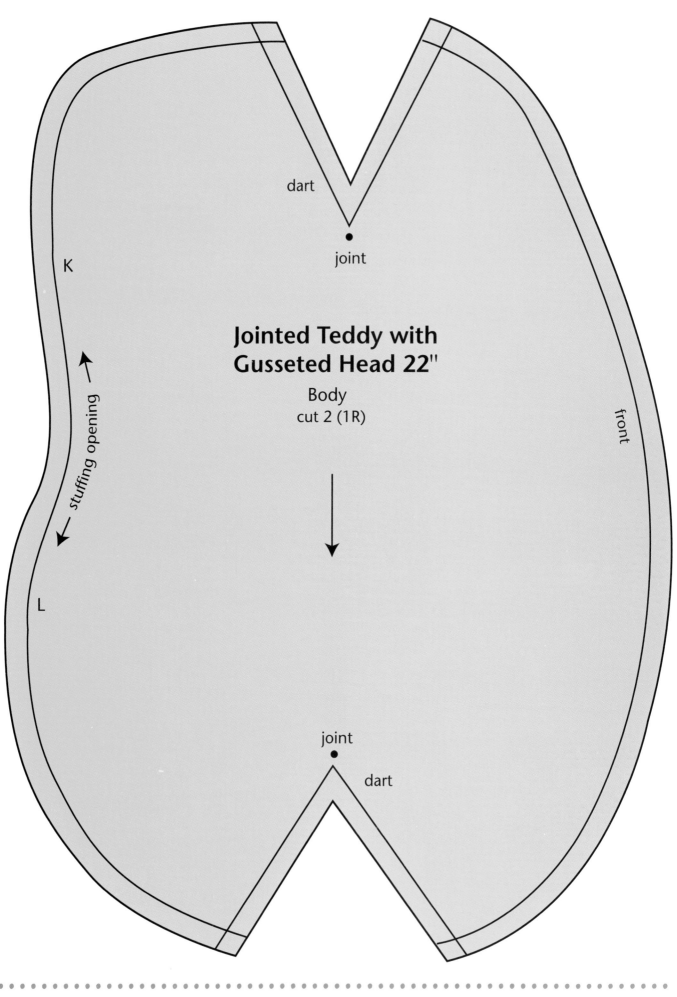

dart

joint

K

stuffing opening

**Jointed Teddy with
Gusseted Head 22"**

Body
cut 2 (1R)

front

L

joint

dart

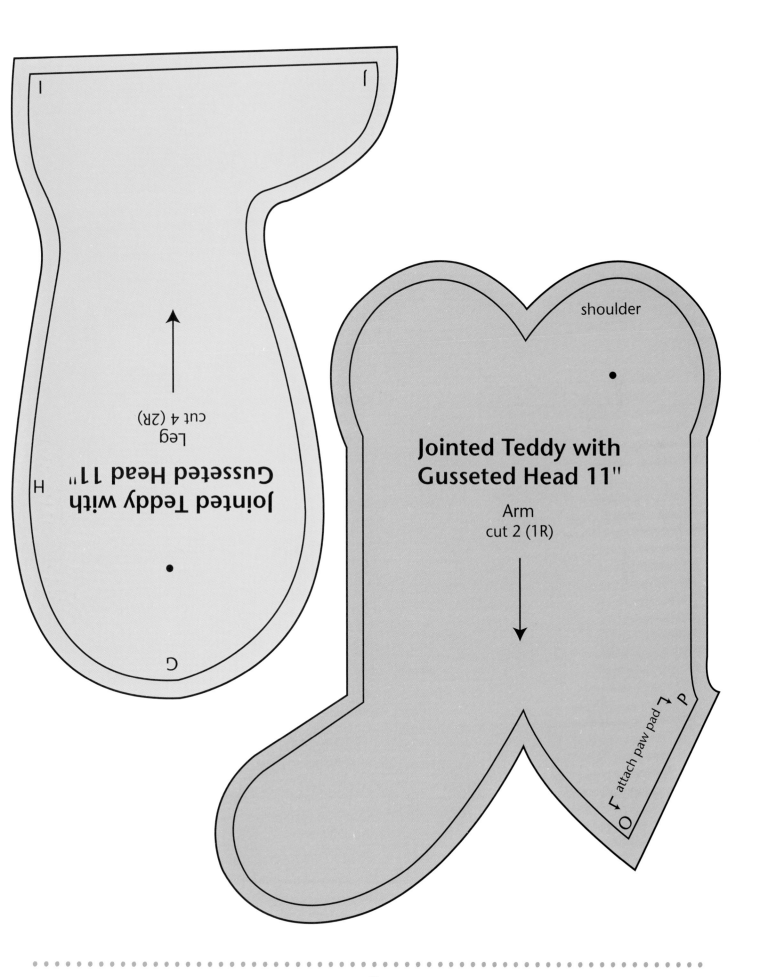

Leg
cut 4 (2R)

Jointed Teddy with
Gusseted Head 11"

H

G

I

I

shoulder

Jointed Teddy with
Gusseted Head 11"

Arm
cut 2 (1R)

attach paw pad

P

O

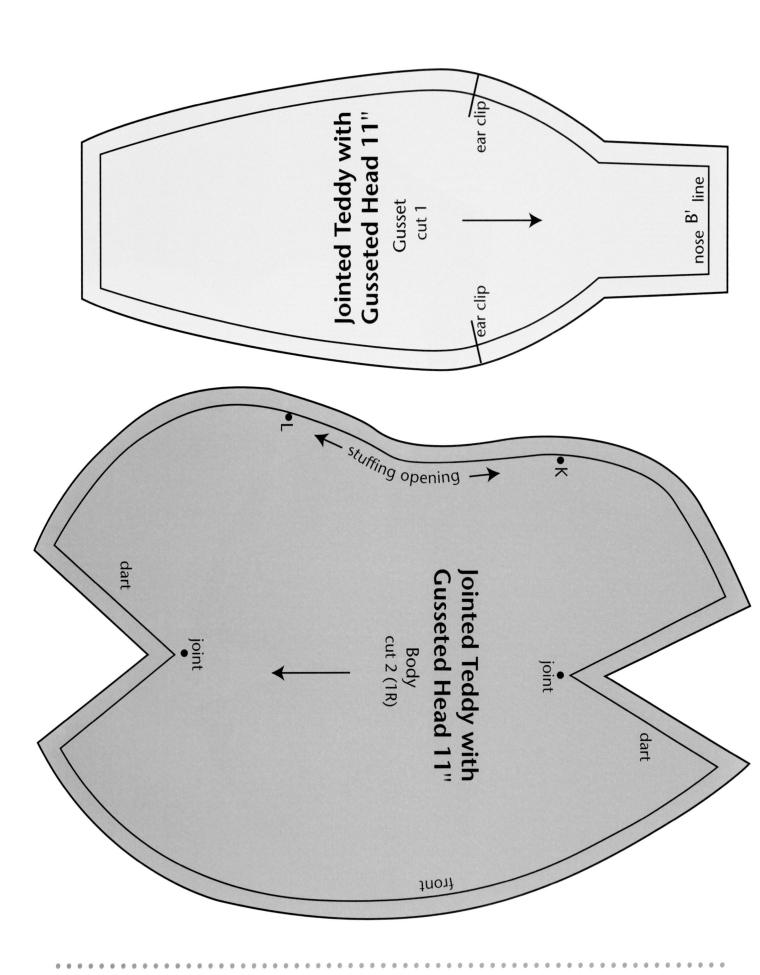

Jointed Teddy with Gusseted Head 11"

Gusset
cut 1

ear clip

ear clip

nose B' line

Jointed Teddy with Gusseted Head 11"

Body
cut 2 (1R)

dart

joint

joint

dart

L

K

stuffing opening

front

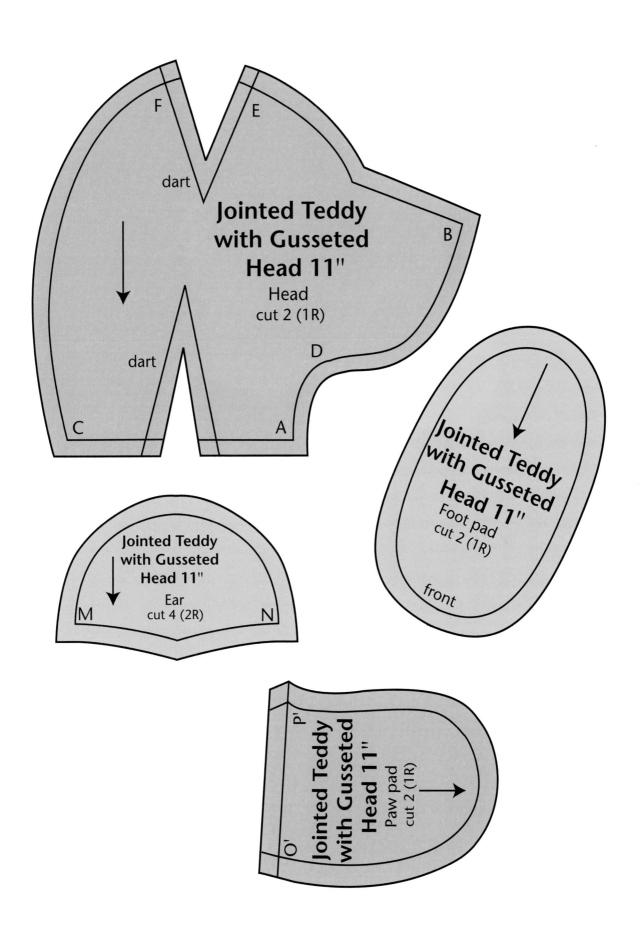

Jointed Teddy with Gusseted Head 11"
Head
cut 2 (1R)

F

E

dart

dart

B

D

A

C

Jointed Teddy with Gusseted Head 11"
Foot pad
cut 2 (1R)

front

Jointed Teddy with Gusseted Head 11"
Ear
cut 4 (2R)

M

N

Jointed Teddy with Gusseted Head 11"
Paw pad
cut 2 (1R)

P'

O'

BluBear Yu, done with multi-jointed limbs

Maria finished the small version of Professor Ted and made his limbs flexible enough to bend freely, especially when tacked as we showed in Project 6, so he could be strung as a marionette. For a day or so, she was content. And then she saw a real, articulated marionette, one whose limbs bend at the middle joint, and she decided she needed one of those. Right away.

Not that I blame her. Multi-jointed dolls have fascinated me since I got a Madame Alexander Cissy, I think it was, in maybe 1954. She not only bent at the knees and elbows, but at the wrists, too. And then Mom gave me the bisque-headed German doll with the jointed composition body she'd had when a girl. Seems some relative in Germany was in the toy business. Once one connects with multi-jointed dolls, or bears, some sort of visceral passion ensues. So I wasn't all that averse to showing Maria how to multi-joint bears so they'll move like real marionettes.

When we were done with BluBear Yu, the jointed gent, I was sorry I'd agreed to "string him along." The joints make him laid back and poseable. Even though he's not a human doll, every time I watched him move and take a pose, something in me went back to that Christmas years ago when I opened the box and fell in love with that Alexander doll. (She still has her original dress, too. I'd better not let Maria meet her. They wear the same size.)

Bear with Multi-Jointed Limbs

- ⅓ yard (.3 m) woven-backed sparse mohair or woven-backed synthetic plush, pile length, ½" (1.3 cm)
- 9" (23 cm) square of paw pad fabric
- Two 9 mm shoe buttons or glass teddy bear eyes*
- Strong thread matching fur (like upholstery thread) or dental floss to insert eyes and finish bear
- Sewing thread to match fabric (like quilting thread)
- Long dollmaking or upholstery needle
- Permanent fine-line marker. Cardboard and tracing paper
- Sewing machine or hand-sewing needles and thimble
- Sewing shears and embroidery scissors
- 18 cotter pins, 1" or 1½" long (2.5 or 3.8 cm). 16 small washers. 12 jointing discs for limbs, diameter 1" (2.5 cm). 2 jointing discs for shoulders, diameter 1" (2.5 cm). 2 jointing discs for hips, diameter 1½" (3.8 cm). 2 jointing discs for head, diameter 1" (2.5 cm).
- Needle-nose pliers (2 pair)
- Liquid seam sealant
- Polyester fiberfill
- Plastic dollmaking pellets
- Stuffing stick
- Perle embroidery cotton. Embroidery needles
- White glue and toothpicks for eyes

Note: If this bear is intended for a child, please embroider the eyes, using black perle cotton.

This chapter will take your bearmaking a step further, literally. The limbs made with these patterns are exactly right if you want to make your teddy into a marionette. They can be used on either of the 11" (28 cm) tall bears we've already made in Projects 5 and 6. For this reason there are only arm and leg pattern pieces with the project. Just substitute the leg and arm patterns given here for the pattern pieces indicated in the original project.

People ask where BluBear Yu got his name. Daughter Jenny-Lynn was visiting when I finished the original BluBear Yu (seen in Project 4). She has a knack for naming bears (she christened Yetta Nother Bear, my first-born).

As I showed her Original, she said: "Nice bear, Mom. You're gonna call him BluBear Yu, aren't you ... like in the Linda Ronstadt song? And she trailed off singing *"Blue Bayou,"* changing lyrics to fit. Now's your chance to bring him to life, so he can dance to his theme song....

Photo 1

Photo 2

Photo 3

Photo 4

Photo 5

Photo 6

INSTRUCTIONS

Pattern preparation: Trace lower leg, upper leg, and upper arm on folded paper, cut out from paper, and use full pattern on fabric. Use ¹/₄" (.6 cm) seam allowances throughout. Construction is done with right sides of fabric facing, unless noted. Other pattern pieces are picked up from an 11" (28 cm) bear.

1 Trace head, body, and limb pieces onto the wrong side of mohair so pile runs down body pieces. Trace paw pads from another 11" bear project onto paw pad fabric. Cut pattern pieces out, using small, sharp scissors, cutting only backing of fabric. Trim fur from seam allowances of all mohair pieces.

2 Fold each of the leg pieces (two upper legs, two lower legs) vertically along center fold line of each piece. Pin each lower leg together from B to A. Sew lower leg section from toe to top front (edge at A to B), leaving rounded area on top (B to C) open (Photo 1).

3 Pin each upper leg together from D to E and E to F and sew from D to E and E to F, leaving bottom (F to G) open (Photo 1). Set aside.

4 Pin paw pad to lower arm from L to M and sew (Photo 2). Backstitch at start and end. The paw pad shown is made from garment-weight suede. A Teflon™-coated foot slides easily over the suede. With right sides together, fold lower arm on fold line and pin each lower arm section from I to J and around to H, leaving top open (Photo 3). Stitch on line around pinned area.

5 Pin and sew each upper arm section from K around curve to H. Stitched arm sections look like Photo 4.

6 Right sides together, pin body pieces (from main pattern) together and stitch on stitch line, but leave back body stuffing opening unstitched for now. Reinforce (sew back and forth several times) at center top, at the spot

marked for head insertion. Clip a slit, ending just a bit inside body area (Photo 5). Dot this hole with seam sealant. Let it dry.

7 Fold foot pads in half on long axis (toe to heel). Mark with pins at front and back of pad. Match foot pad center front with center front seam of lower leg. Match center back foot pad with center back seam. Pin pad into foot, easing around curves. It is easiest to pin on each side from front and back, working towards the center. You may want to baste foot pad into lower leg. Sew foot pads to lower legs.

8 Clip seam allowances at curves on arms and legs, but don't clip stitches.

9 Make head as described in bear project 5 or 6. Set it aside.

Photo 7

Photo 8

Photo 9

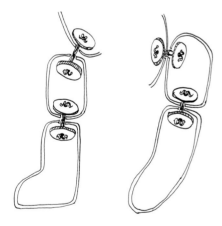

Photo 10

Photo 11

Photo 12

Diagram 1: Joint location in multi-jointed limbs.

10 Turn limb parts right-side out (Photo 6). Note: These limbs will be used in a marionette. Joints are at top of limb for lots of movement. If you prefer (as for most normal bears you would), you can make joints at side of limbs instead; see Project 5, Jointed Bear, for techniques. Diagram 1 shows location of limb joints in multi-jointed bear.

11 We will be making a joint at top and bottom of upper arm. To begin jointing arms, use point of embroidery scissors or awl to pierce a hole in the center top of each upper arm (Photo 7). Dot a bit of seam sealant on the hole.

12 Slip a small washer over both legs of a cotter pin (Photo 8, right). Then slip another cotter pin through the head of the first cotter pin, joining them.

13 Add a second washer and from the outside, poke a cotter pin into hole you made with the awl at the top of the upper arm (Photo 9). Scooch up sides of upper arm and slip a disc joint onto the cotter pin inside the upper arm.

14 Using needle-nose pliers, make a crown joint to hold the disc inside the top of the upper arm (Photo 10). See Tips and Techniques for how to make a crown joint (p. 110).

15 Turn upper arm inside out. Fold over bottom hem of $1/4$" (.6 cm) on upper arm. Using strong thread (dental floss or upholstery thread), run a gathering line on folded-over edge (Photo 11). Turn right-side out and stuff upper arm lightly with polyester fiberfill.

16 Make a crown joint on another disc. Insert cotter pin into top loop of crown joint (Photo 12, left).

Photo 13

Photo 14

Photo 15

Photo 16

Photo 17

Photo 18

17 With unbent cotter pin dangling out, insert disc joint into bottom of upper arm (Photo 13). Tug on gathering thread to pull up gathering stitches around cotter pin.

18 With cotter pin sticking out of limb, hand-stitch with strong thread around bottom of upper arm to close securely (Photo 14). You now have a joint at top and bottom of upper arm.

19 Next we make a crown joint that will go inside the top of the lower arm. Grasp the unbent cotter pin of the bottom of the upper arm with needle-nose pliers. By glomming onto the cotter pin with the needle-nose pliers, you create a bit of wiggle room between the 2 halves of the bear's arm. The pliers barrier forces you to leave this space (Photo 15). Slip a washer and joint disc onto cotter pin, atop pliers. Bend arms of cotter pin outward and, holding onto joint with first pair of pliers, make crown joint atop disc with second pliers (Photo 16). Set upper arm aside.

20 Take lower arm and stuff paw firmly to wrist, nicely rounding it. Pour some pellets into the arm to make it scrunchy; not too many. Top with a bit of fiberfill to keep everything in place (Photo 17). Using strong thread or dental floss, run a line of gathering stitches around open end of lower arm (Photo 18). Pull gathers a bit to round top.

Photo 19

Photo 20

Photo 21

Photo 22

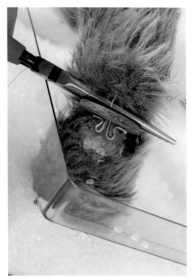
Photo 23

Photo 24

21 Now, slip the disc you added in Step 19 into the top of the lower arm. This is why you created a space with the pliers, so the lower arm could move easily. Pull on the dental floss to draw the gathers together tightly. Sew back and forth with strong thread to secure stitches (Photo 19) to close the opening.

22 The very tops of bear's upper arms look like Photo 20. Slip a second cotter pin through cotter pin on top of each arm. This pin will go into body later. Set arms aside.

23 Stuff foot area of lower leg firmly to ankle with fiberfill. Top it with pellets. Run a gathering line at top of lower leg with dental floss or strong thread.

24 Make a crown joint onto a disc. Attach a second cotter pin to head of bent cotter pin. Insert in top of lower leg so second (unbent) cotter pin pokes through to outside. Sew up opening in top of lower leg around cotter pin.

25 Add a joint disc and bend protruding arms of pin into a crown joint (Photos 21 and 22).

26 Grasping area between joints with pliers, guide disc from top of lower leg joint into open part of upper leg (Photo 23). Pull up dental floss gathering thread so joint is surrounded by the leg.

27 Tug firmly on gathering thread. You may need to fiddle a bit with gathers to make joint area smooth and the fit snug. Stitch upper leg closed around joint disc with sturdy stitches (Photo 24).

Photo 25

Photo 26

Photo 27

Photo 28

30 Slip small washer onto cotter pin sticking out of top of leg (Photo 25). Making sure front of foot points forward on body, insert cotter pin into correct body hole, and add disc on cotter pin inside body. Make a crown joint inside body (Photo 26). Finished leg joint at hip can be seen in Photo 27. Heads of two connected cotter pins, seen between two washers, allow for easy, floppy movement.

31 Joint arms to body as you did legs. This bear's set to dance and he's not yet stuffed (Photo 28).

32 Stuff body with fiberfill and pellets; see stuffing section in Tips and Techniques for details. Close body stuffing seam with ladder stitch, using strong thread.

28 See Project 5 (Step 24) for making arm and leg insertion holes in body. Photo 25 shows disc on outside, being used to plan limb placement.

29 To attach head, insert cotter pin through slit you've cut and reinforced at top of body, add disc inside and joint head to body, making crown joint.

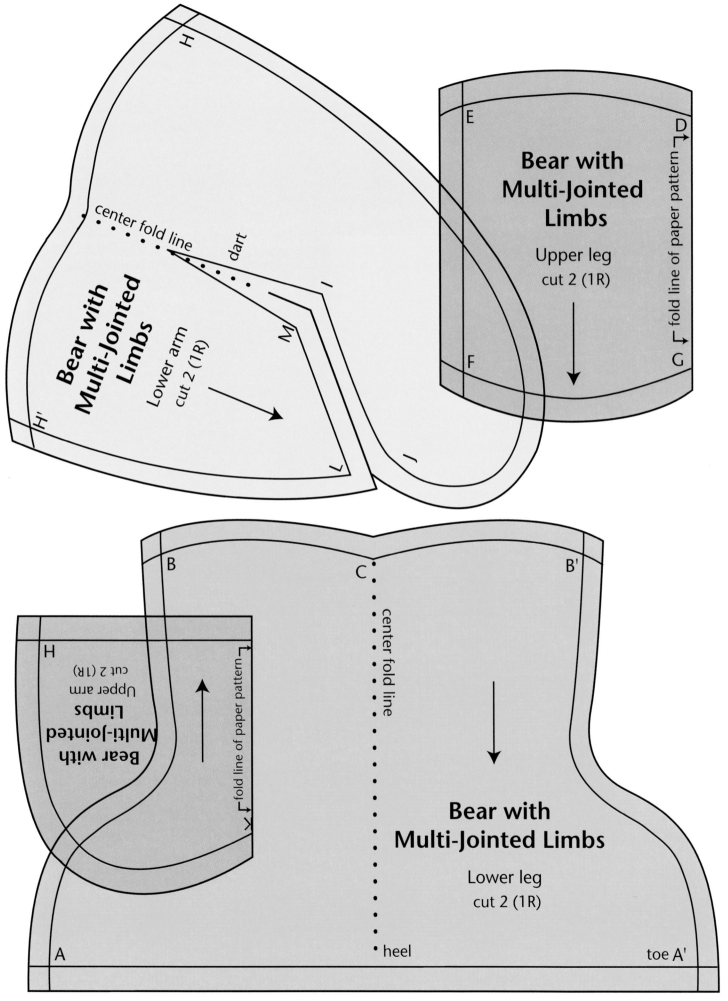

Bear with Multi-Jointed Limbs

Lower arm
cut 2 (1R)

center fold line

dart

H'

H

Bear with Multi-Jointed Limbs

Upper leg
cut 2 (1R)

E

D

F

G

fold line of paper pattern

Bear with Multi-Jointed Limbs

Upper arm
cut 2 (1R)

H

fold line of paper pattern

B

C

B'

center fold line

Bear with Multi-Jointed Limbs

Lower leg
cut 2 (1R)

A

heel

toe A'

71

*W*here do marionettes hang out when not performing? Nicholas had the answer: a time-out stand, customized to fit the personality of each character. One rainy day he phoned me a list of supplies to get at the crafts store so we could build a couple. By the time I arrived on campus, he'd scrounged tools and transformed the sewing table into a workshop.

   We soon discovered neither of us wielded a nimble saw ... or any other tool. But it didn't matter. As the sewing room got dusted with an irregular coat of sawdust, the stands and poles for the bears began taking on shape and personality. When we got through the raw-wood-glued-together stage, a funny thing happened. Our potential actors barged through the open doorway, climbed onto the table and took over customizing operations. I began to look forward to seeing what they might do on stage.

BluBear Yu and Professor Ted marionettes take a break on their stands.

BluBear Yu involved in gluing activities.

Marionette Stands

You can make one of these in an afternoon on your kitchen table or workbench. Everything you need comes from your local craft or hardware store. Just follow the bears, step by step, as they get to work. If they can do it, so can you!

- Ruler (a metal one is nice)
- Pencil
- One rectangular wooden base or plaque shape, 6" x 8" (15 x 20 cm). One circular wooden base or plaque, 6" (15 cm) in diameter. These sizes aren't exact; find ones that fit the bear you're working with.
- 2 decorative, ornamental wooden scroll shapes (optional)
- 3 wooden screw hole pegs
- 3 dowels: $1/4$" (.6 cm), $1/2$" (1.3 cm), and $5/8$" (1.6 cm) in diameter; all 36" (91 cm) long
- Miter box and miter saw, or saw and C clamps
- Narrow metal file with tapered front
- Wood glue
- Rubber bands
- Drill and drill bits $1/4$" (.6 cm), $1/8$" (.3 cm), and $1/2$" (1.3 cm) in diameter
- Awl
- Two $1\,1/4$ to $1\,1/2$" long (3.2 to 3.8 cm) wood screws
- Carpenter's tape measure
- Screw driver
- Wooden decorations for stand (alphabet letters or shapes)
- Brown pencil
- Two screw eyes
- Sandpaper
- Protection for your work table, e.g., $1/4$" (.6 cm) plywood or rotary cutting mat
- Water-based wood stains or paint in 2 contrasting colors, if desired
- Paintbrush or sponge for stain
- Paper towels

Photo 1

Photo 2

Photo 3

Photo 4

INSTRUCTIONS

It's almost as easy, fast, and economical to make two stands as one. You'll probably find different shaped wooden pieces from the ones we used. Use imagination and ingenuity.

1 Mark a line across the diameter of the circular wooden plaque. Using saw and miter box, or similar setup, cut plaque in half (Photo 1). Smooth the edges with sandpaper or a metal file.

2 Select a decorative shape to fit. Apply wood glue and make a sandwich of the pieces with the glue inside. Wipe edges clean. Secure with rubber bands. Allow to dry (Photo 2).

3 On the quarter-circle line of the semicircular wooden piece, about an inch (2.5 cm) in from the edge, make a pencil mark (Photo 3). Drill a hole through both thicknesses of wood with the 1/2" (1.3 cm) drill bit, or widen hole to 1/2" (1.3 cm). This will fit the tall part of the stand.

4 Use a tapered metal file to smooth insides of hole (Photo 4).

5 For each marionette stand, cut an 8" (20 cm) length of 5/8" dowel (1.6 cm), a 7" (18 cm) length of 1/4" (.6 cm) dowel, and 18" (46 cm) of 1/2" (1.3 cm) dowel. The 5/8" dowel will be the handle, the 1/4" dowel will be the piece that holds the strings, and the 1/2" (1.3 cm) dowel will be the stand.

Photo 5

Photo 6

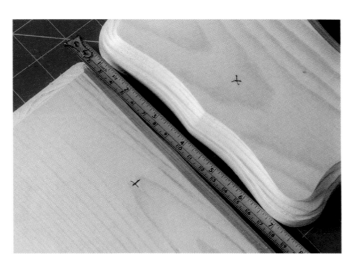

Photo 7

6 About 2" (5 cm) from end of the ⁵/₈" dowel, make a pencil mark. Use awl to make a starter hole there for drill and, using ¹/₄" drill bit, drill through dowel to create a hole the diameter of the thinnest dowel (Photo 5). Use tapered metal file to smooth and enlarge hole to size.

7 Make pencil mark at center point of ¹/₄" diameter dowel and slip dowel through hole in ⁵/₈" dowel to see if it fits. Remove.

8 About ¹/₂" (1.3 cm) below hole in ⁵/₈" dowel, 90 degrees around from hole, make a mark with awl. Drill a hole through it with ⁵/₈" drill (Photo 6). Use tapered file to round out top of hole so the wooden bead can sit there. Glue the ¹/₄" dowel inside ⁵/₈" dowel, centering it so an equal length sticks out on each side. Set it aside.

9 About 1¹/₂" (3.8 cm) in from the center of stand bottom, make pencil mark (Photo 7). Drill hole through base at pencil mark to fit 1¹/₂" long (3.8 cm) screw.

Photo 8

Photo 9

Photo 10

Photo 11

10 Use awl to start hole in center at top and bottom of 1/2" (1.3 cm) diameter dowel and drill into it to a depth of 1/2" (1.3 cm) at both ends of dowel (Photo 8). From the back of base bottom, insert wood screw through base into 1/2" (1.3 cm) dowel, making dowel fast to base. Dowel should be strong, not wobbly (Photo 9).

11 Drill hole in stand top and attach top of stand to 1/2" (1.3 cm) dowel in the same way. Unfinished stands look like Photo 10. Use sandpaper to smooth them for finishing.

12 Glue screw hole cover over screw attaching top to dowel and at each corner edge of top (Photo 11).

13 Stain or paint base. Staining with water-based stains is easy. Glomp stain onto wood, and spread it out. A thin coat looks best. You can always do a second. Too thick a coat hides wood grain (which is a good reason not to use paint). Stain handle for marionette and decorations for the stand. It's nice to make each stand special, indicating which bear owns it. Use a decorative plaque for the top if you wish. Let stain dry (Photo 12).

Photo 12

Photo 13

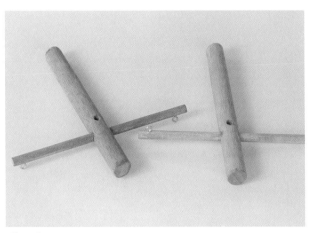

Photo 14

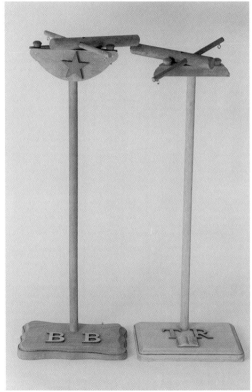

Photo 15

14 Figure out where you want trim to go on base and top of stand and glue decorations and trim to stand. Use rubber bands, if necessary, to hold in place while glue dries.

15 To make holders for marionette strings to slip through, use awl or fine drill on cross piece to make holes to attach screw eyes into bottom of cross piece (Photo 13). Photo 14 shows a top view of completed marionette handles. Photo 15 shows the completed stands and marionette handles. Next project: Marionette-stringing!

BluBear Yu practices for a dancing role.

While the stain dried on the wooden parts of the marionettes' rigging, Carrie reclaimed the sewing table and produced a tea experience. And I don't use the word "produced" without reason. The better I get to know the Björn clan, the more I'm convinced their lives are one huge stage play.

Professor Ted followed his astute academic nose and, seeing the foodish experience in progress, joined in with gusto. Besides being an expert on the plots and stars of every movie done since Edison, he's an expert in arctology, an arcane, age-old discipline rediscovered in 1995, centering on techniques for teddy bear construction.

Professor Ted had most definite ideas on how best to string a marionette. After we swept the crumbs off the sewing table, the Master got to work with hugeish dollmaking needles and a reel of fishing line from his last trip to the fishing section of his favorite store. (You might consider a trip to a fishing supply shop when making bears, especially little ones. Turn your brain sideways and look at the threads and feathers and gear for fly-tying. You'll never look at it again as merely stuff to throw into the water.)

Our potential stars weathered the operation well. They seemed to gain balletic skill and grace with insertion of their invisible strings. And Ted seemed most pleased with his smaller duplicate: so much so he announced he was going to use that item in the theatrical opus.

Stringing Your Marionette

- Marionette from Project 6 or 7
- Marionette stand, marionette handle (see Project 8)
- Small wooden bead to fit hole in handle
- Scissors
- 30-pound test monofilament fishing line
- Long dollmaker's needle. Large embroidery needle
- Carpenter's tape measure
- Needle-nose pliers
- Elastic yarn
- Small screw eyes (the kind for picture wire)

Marionettes need strings to bring them to life. Ted and BluBear Yu will help you learn easy stringing techniques. It's time to get started. The show must go on!

Professor Ted resting his feet between scenes.

Photo 1

Photo 2

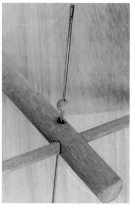

Photo 3

Photo 4

Photo 5

Photo 6

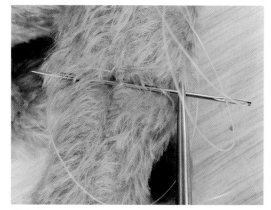

Photo 7

INSTRUCTIONS

1 Lay out marionette, fishing line, scissors, needle, handle and bead on table.

2 Align your marionette bear along pole of stand. Measure from top of stand to top of bear's head. The bear in Photo 1 stands about 6" (15 cm) below top of stand. Cut a length of fishing line double the length from top of stand to the bear's head.

3 Thread a long dollmaker's needle with one end of the cut fishing line. Knot the other end. Insert needle at base of bear's head. Sew through head, coming out at top. Continue sewing through hole in marionette handle and through hole in wooden bead (Photo 2).

4 Return needle through hole in marionette handle (Photo 3), through bear's head again, exiting where you began. Take a stitch or two to fasten thread at spot needle entered head. If you pull up on the bead with the marionette handle, bear's head moves.

5 Measure bear from top of stand to wrist, with arm down (Photo 4). This bear measures about 13" (33 cm).

6 Measure from top of stand to bottom with carpenter's measuring tape (Photo 5). If you used measurements in Project 8, this stand measures 18" (46 cm). Add this measurement, plus 2" (5 cm), to arm length measurement. Here it would be 20" + 13" (51 + 33 cm). Cut two lengths of fishing line this length.

7 Thread one of the lengths of fish line through a needle, knotting the end. Begin attaching marionette strings to back of legs at knee-bend. Depending upon construction of your bear, this could be at either of the following spots: (1) If your bear has double-jointed legs, at back of lower leg, just below joint. (2) If your bear has normal legs, attach them at the knee break. Photo 6 shows needle coming through a regular leg at knee level. Pull the thread securely, and take several long stitches parallel to the knee joint. A pair of pliers helps push needle through limb (Photo 7).

8 Push needle through to front of leg at lower end of knee level. Photo 8 shows multi-jointed leg.

9 Thread needle through the screw eye on marionette handle that is on same side as leg, and then into paw of bear (Photo 9). Insert needle at one of two spots: at bear's wrist, angling it towards outside of wrist (Photo 10) or halfway down paw (Photo 11).

10 Take a couple of long, sturdy stitches at bottom of paw where needle emerges (Photo 12), if you stitch into paw. Secure with a dab of seam sealant.

11 Lay top of marionette stand upside down on table. Attach screw eye to underside of top of stand, at rear (Photo 13).

12 Thread 6" (15 cm) length of elastic yarn through screw eye and knot the ends together to make a loop.

13 Use this elastic to secure marionette's handle to stand, slipping elastic loop over bead on handle (Photo 14).

The bear stand allows marionette to be ready, eagerly awaiting his turn on stage, or he can use it as his personal performance place and do high kicks.

Photo 8

Photo 9

Photo 10

Photo 11

Photo 12

Photo 13

Photo 14

Maria with freshly stitched mini hand puppet.

The date for the Teddy Bear Marionette and Puppet Extravaganza was fast approaching. Professor Ted came up with a better-than-expected script about the history of Teddy Bear University (TBU), centering on the love story of its founders, Rosa BonneBear and his distant relative BlaBjörn (BluBear Yu).

Maria decided she was musical director; she said that each time BlaBjörn and Rosa "got together" on stage, it would be to his theme song, the one made famous years ago by singer Linda Ronstadt. She decided this on the same day she made the decision the big, human-sized puppets were out of the show, to be replaced with handsome, handy bear-sized ones she could manipulate without any help from the likes of me.

"No offense," she said, "but this is a Bears-for-Bears Thing. You understand." And she scrounged in my stash of mohair until she found a length of shortish, blue fabric just right for making a Maria-sized puppet.

She and Nicky shared the tasks. Maria sewed while Nick cut out, stuffed and embroidered. By that afternoon, both the pink and the blue hand puppet were done, just in time for tea, which Carrie ferried into the sewing room on a hand-painted metal tray that matched the samovar and teapot from Arkhangelsk.

Carrie had been so busy with the costumes for the theatre, and with all the publicity stills she'd been doing of the cast, we seldom saw her in the sewing room. In fact, I rather imagined she'd lost interest in "our" end of the production. As usual, I was wrong. When she laid eyes on the bear-sized puppetlike versions of Rosa and Blue, she put down the tea tray, and put on the puppets, one on each paw.

"I'd wondered what part I was going to play in the show," she said, bopping little Rosa's head up and down. And here it is ... just waiting for me. Thanks, kids. And you made them just my size."

Maria and Nicholas stuff a bear puppet's head

82

Mini Hand Puppet, Style 1

- ⅛ yard (.1 m) woven-backed mohair or synthetic pile fabric. A good pile length is ¼" (.6 cm)
- Sewing thread to match fabric
- Dental floss or strong (upholstery) thread for inserting eyes
- Dollmaker's needle. Large-eyed embroidery needle
- Two 6 mm glass teddy bear eyes or black onyx beads for eyes*
- Perle cotton or embroidery floss for embroidering nose and claws
- Polyester fiberfill or cotton
- Sewing machine or hand-sewing needles and thimble
- Stuffing stick
- Small, sharp scissors
- Seam sealant (optional)
- Fine-line permanent marker
- White glue and toothpick for eyes

If making this bear for a child, please embroider eyes with black perle cotton.

Are your bears clamoring to put on a show like Maria and Nicholas? Or do you just want to keep a bit of show business in your pocket? The little bear puppets in this project and the following one are eager to perform; they come in handy on long flights, train trips or camping expeditions. These little guys just fit the paws of the cast of characters in our story or onto a couple of your fingers.

A gallery of mini hand puppets (front row) are visited by their tiny teddy cousins

Photo 1

Photo 2

Photo 3

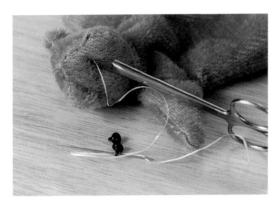

Photo 4

Photo 5

INSTRUCTIONS

Construction is done with right sides of fabric facing and $1/8$" (.3 cm) seam allowances, unless otherwise noted.

1 Cut out body front pattern from folded paper. Unfold and use whole pattern to trace on back of fabric. Draw a body front and back and two head back pieces (1R) onto fabric with marker. Reserve a rectangle of fabric big enough for two head fronts, nose to nose. Cut out body and head backs along drawn lines with small, sharp scissors.

2 Cut out a rectangle twice as wide as the head front and fold it. Draw one head front onto fabric rectangle so nose front is on fold. Sew along line from forehead to nose (A to B), backstitching at start and finish (Photo 1).

3 Sew jaw line of bear on head front, from folded nose line to neck (B to C), backstitching start and finish. Trim head front seam allowance just outside stitching.

4 Pin unsewn parts of head fronts together. Cut out rest of head front, top layer first, along drawn line; then cut bottom layer, using top layer as a pattern. Unpin and set aside.

5 Sew head back pieces together on center back seam (A´ to G).

6 With right sides of fabric together, pin head front to body front at neck and pin head back to body back at neck. Sew head front and head back to body pieces at neck.

7 On body front piece, trim paw pad area fur with small, sharp scissors. (Adding a separate paw pad is optional.)

8 Pin body front to back, finger-pressing neck seam allowances open. Sew body front to back, leaving a 2" (5 cm) seam open along at bottom of one side seam (Photo 2).

9 Zigzag stitch raw edge of hem at bottom, finger-pressing side seam allowances flat before you do. Pin up $1/4$" (.6 cm) hem and stitch.

10 Clip seam allowances at curves all around puppet, especially at armholes, neck sides, and the round area around ears and top of head. Pin unsewn area at side seam closed and sew, backstitching at each end.

11 Using stuffing stick, turn puppet right-side out. Photo 3 shows four stuffing sticks useful for stuffing small bears. Once puppet is right-side out, use stick to round out nose, ears and paws. Sew along ear stitch line, across top of head, and along second ear stitch line to shape ears.

Photo 6

Photo 7

Photo 8

Photo 9

12 Using stuffing stick, stuff head and paws partway with polyester fiberfill or cotton. Cotton makes a nice, sturdy stuffing. Stuff nose area of head first, inserting small wads of fluff wound around stuffing stick. Leave enough room for your fingers to fit inside puppet.

13 At bear's eye level, sew back and forth through nose between eye sockets with upholstery thread or dental floss, leaving some thread dangling on needle. Just behind this spot, insert point of scissors (Photo 4). Make a hole where you want eye. Seal hole with seam sealant. Allow to dry. Repeat on other side of head. Thread a 5 mm or 6 mm glass teddy bear eye, or a black onyx bead, onto needle.

14 Sew through snout to other side, emerging in eye hole. Thread glass eye or onyx bead onto needle (Photo 5).

Sew again through nose area, catching loop at back of eye again with tip of needle. Repeat. Pull thread taut. This should sink eye loop into hole. But don't pull too taut; you'll need to poke needle through eye loops again. Now poke needle, starting from eye hole, up through head, emerging at ear area on opposite side of head, at seam between ear and head.

15 Insert needle into center ear back, about $1/8$" (.3 cm) up from seam between ear and head. Take a stitch. Insert needle into spot needle exited on back. Poke needle to front, and emerge at eye level, catching the loop of eye in it (Photo 6). Sew needle through bridge of nose, catching eye loop at other eye, and poke needle up through head, emerging at ear on opposite side of head. Repeat process, exiting needle through nose. Clip thread ends.

16 Mark top and bottom edges of nose with pins. Outline area of nose with perle cotton or embroidery floss (Project 7). Using satin stitch, fill in nose area, starting in middle, sewing one stitch above and one stitch below center, repeating this procedure until you reach outside framing stitch.

17 Refer to Making Faces section of book for detailed how-to on completing facial embroidery (Photo 8).

18 Embroider four claws on each paw (Photo 9).

19 Use toothpick to stick some white glue behind each eye; let dry.

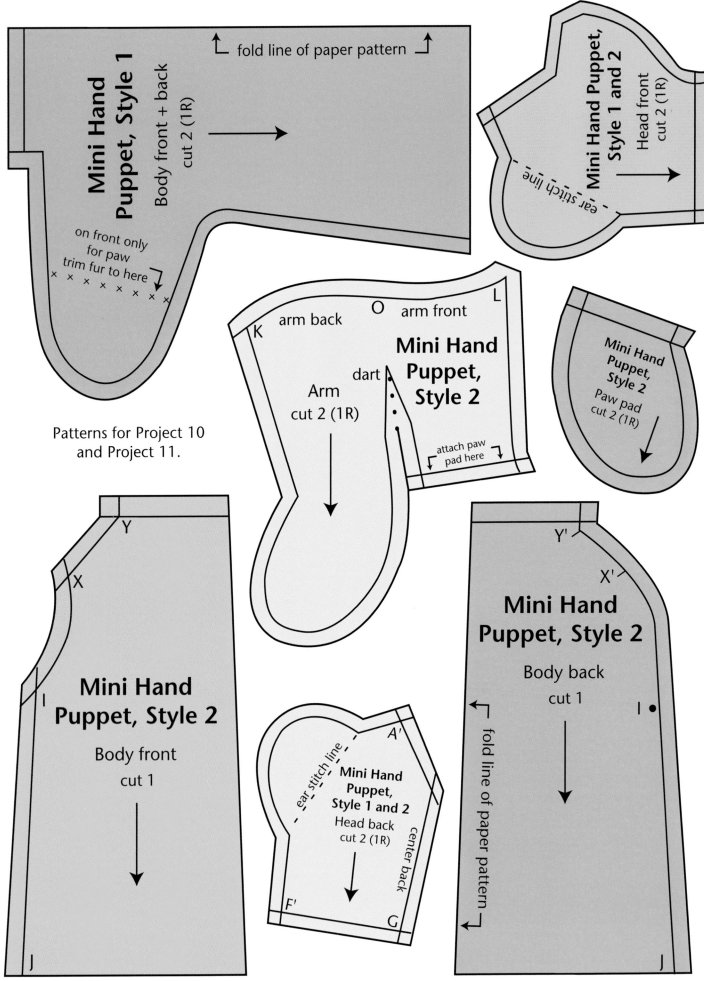

Mini Hand Puppet, Style 1
Body front + back
cut 2 (1R)

fold line of paper pattern

on front only
for paw
trim fur to here
× × × × × × × × ×

**Mini Hand Puppet,
Style 1 and 2**
Head front
cut 2 (1R)

ear stitch line

Patterns for Project 10
and Project 11.

arm back   O   arm front

K   L

**Mini Hand
Puppet,
Style 2**

dart

Arm
cut 2 (1R)

attach paw
pad here

**Mini Hand
Puppet,
Style 2**

Paw pad
cut 2 (1R)

Y

X

I

**Mini Hand
Puppet, Style 2**

Body front

cut 1

J

**Mini Hand Puppet,
Style 1 and 2**

Head back
cut 2 (1R)

ear stitch line

A'

center back

F'

G

Y'

X'

**Mini Hand
Puppet, Style 2**

Body back
cut 1

I

fold line of paper pattern

J

Nicholas visits with a mini Nicholas hand puppet.

*C*arrie and I were sitting at the kitchen table, going over my notes for the book and sipping some of the best Russian tea I've had since last summer on a midnight train to Nyandoma, Russia. The twins and I, along with their Uncle Greg, flew from Maine to Arkhangelsk, thence to Sweden, so they could search for their roots. On the way home from Russia, we spent six days in Sweden. We visited Sigtuna, Sweden's oldest town, where the twins' grandparents, the Rev. Dr. Carl Oskar Björn and Anastasia Nikolaevna Medved, met one midsummer night and fell in love.

We visited Husqvarna, where they make sewing machines which can embroider the entire 29 letters of the Swedish alphabet (which is why both Maria and I bought ours) and spent time in Stockholm looking for places my grandmother, Maria Alma Oskara Holm, lived when she was a girl.

I got to know Nicky pretty well on that trip. And sometimes I wonder how the twins hatched together. Funny thing: he knows exactly how Maria operates, yet he never complains. He says it's a sister thing, meaning I should get to know both sisters before I write the final story.

Actually, I'd been planning on doing just that. At the moment, Jenny-Lynn's doing the most wonderful work with heirloom sewing and embroideries, and she's invited me to come for an audience at the shop as she gets it ready for the opening.

I asked Carrie if she really was going to glom onto the puppets for the show. A sneaky smile curved around her face. "What do you think? Nicky's been asking for you," she said. "Would you mind bringing a tea tray with you when you go to the sewing room?"

When I got there, Nicky'd figured out how to reduce the big Style 2 hand puppet and was chugging away at a new project as if his life depended on it.

Mini Hand Puppet, Style 2

- ¹⁄₈ yard (.11 m) woven-backed mohair or synthetic pile fabric. A good pile length is ¹⁄₄" (.6 cm)
- 4" (10 cm) square of paw pad material
- Sewing thread to match mohair
- Dental floss or strong (upholstery) thread for inserting eyes
- Two 5 mm or 6 mm glass eyes or black onyx beads for eyes*
- Perle cotton or embroidery floss for embroidering nose and claws
- Polyester fiberfill or cotton
- Dollmaker's needle. Large-eyed embroidery needle
- Sewing machine, or hand-sewing needles and thimble
- Stuffing stick
- Small, sharp scissors
- Fine-line permanent marker
- White glue and toothpick
- Seam sealant (optional)

*If making this bear for a child, please embroider eyes with black perle cotton.

When she saw the puppet versions of Rosa and BluBear Yu, Maria decided it was high time to make important puppets, meaning ones that looked like her. Nicholas knew better than to argue, so he got to work. He thought he was making a puppet to look like himself. Maria knew it was a puppet of herself. Nicholas knew his twin, so he sat down and made another.

Maria waves hello with a mini hand puppet of Nicholas.

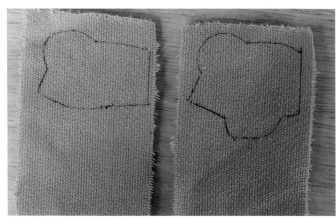

Photo 1

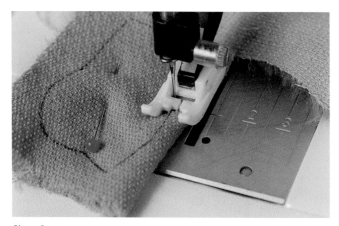

Photo 2

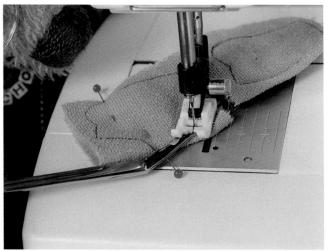

Photo 3

Photo 4

INSTRUCTIONS

Construction is done with right sides of fabric facing and 1/8" (.3 cm) seam allowances, unless noted. The pattern pieces for Project 11 are given with Project 10, as the head and paw pad patterns are exactly the same for both projects (see page 86).

1 Cut out body front and back patterns on folded paper and open out for full patterns.

2 Arrange puppet pattern pieces on back of mohair so pile runs down body. Leave enough extra for a rectangle twice the size of each head piece. Arrange paw pad pattern on paw pad fabric. Trace around pieces with permanent marker.

3 Cut out body pieces from fabric. Cut out rectangles from fur for head pieces and fold each in half. Trace around each head piece on its rectangle with permanent marker as shown in Photo 1, leaving room for second piece.

4 Fold head back rectangle in half with right side of fur in. Sew center back seam from A' to G, backstitching at start and end to reinforce (Photo 2).

5 Fold head front rectangle in half on nose line. Sew head front from A (forehead) to B (nose), on drawn line, backstitching at start and end. Sew head front from neck (C) to nose fold (B) on drawn line, backstitching at ends (Photo 3).

6 Pin back of head through both thicknesses. Cut out head back on drawn lines in top layer. Using cut out part as pattern, cut out the second layer of head back (Photo 4). Do the same for the head front.

7 Open out sewn pieces. Finger-press seam allowances flat. Pin front and back of head together from top of head (A) around ears and along side seams to neck (F). Backstitching at ends, sew front and back of head together, leaving bottom (neck opening) unstitched.

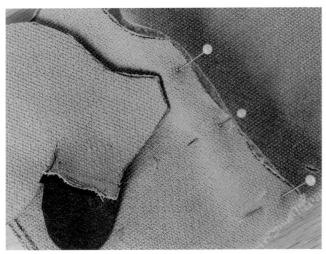

Photo 5

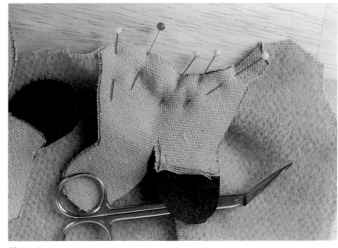

Photo 6

Photo 7

8 Clip seam allowances at curves. Using stuffing stick, turn head right-side out, rounding ears and snout. Backstitching at start and end, sew diagonally across ear on stitch line and across top of head, then diagonally across second ear, to distinguish ear from head.

9 Pin and sew paw pads to each arm (Photo 5).

10 Sew front and back of body together on one shoulder from X to Y.

11 Pin and sew arm to armhole on sewn-up shoulder of puppet as shown (Photo 6), aligning O at center top of arm with shoulder seam where front and back body meet. Sewn-on paw pad should face the front of the body.

12 Fold arm on center line so paws line up, and sew arm sides to each other, tapering seam allowance into fold on unsewn arm side (Photo 7), finger-pressing paw pad and wrist seam allowances flat.

13 Sew up second shoulder of puppet body as in Step 10 and repeat steps 11 and 12 for second arm.

14 Sew sides of body front to back from J to I on both sides.

15 Pin bottom hem of puppet up 1/4" (.6 cm), finger-pressing side seam allowances flat. Zigzag-stitch hem into place.

16 Using sturdy (upholstery) thread or dental floss, gather puppet head's neck. Draw up thread to fit neckline. Match

head sides to shoulder side seams, with nose facing front body piece and place inside body, right sides facing. Baste head to body (Photo 8).

17 To get a jump start for machine stitching the head to body, place a scrap of fabric under your sewing foot next to the basted body and head (Photo 9). Stitch across the scrap, continuing sewing with the puppet's neck seam (Photo 10). Zigzag neck seam to finish.

18 Using stuffing tool (Photo 11), stuff head and paws of puppet with fiberfill, but leave room for fingers.

19 Attach the eyes, make the face (Photo 12 and 13), and embroider the claws as for Mini-Hand Puppet Style 1.

Photo 8

Photo 9

Photo 10

Photo 11

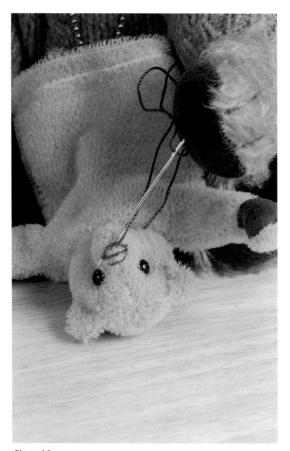

Photo 12

Photo 13

Tiny teddies Nicholas, BluBear Yu, Rosa BonneBear, and Maria pose for the camera

*I*t's been a couple of weeks since the show. It ran something like eight performances, matinees, and — to my total surprise — got rave reviews. Now the show's done, Maria's after me to take her someplace ... again. These bears are the best excuse I've had in a long time to travel. They've got relatives, it seems, in every corner of the globe. As I write this, they're putting together a schedule of "wanna-goes." So far, it says: "New York, England, Boston, Sweden, and another trip to see Anastasia in Arkhangelsk, please." These bears like reruns. I told them I wouldn't mind a trip to Wales to see whence came their Grandpa Merlin's clan.

The other night when I came to work with Professor Ted on the final bits of this book, I came up with a surprise: travel bears. These guys are just right to bring anywhere. They fit in a pocket, a purse, a zippered pack around your waist. They don't eat much, but have a penchant for tea and marzipan fruit, especially at Christmastime, when they have great fun climbing into and out of Christmas stockings, trees, and decorations. Don't tell Maria, but they're one of my favorite sizes of bear. Once you cradle one of these guys in your palm and sorta wiggle its limbs around, you'll see, incontrovertibly, that bears do come to life.

If you need real evidence, genuine artifacts to convince you that all that's happened in this book is true, I recommend you take a page from Maria's script: come do a little traveling in the general direction of the Central Lakes District of Maine (the state whose slogan is: Maine ... the way life ought to be).

Just down Route 202 from Winthrop you'll find the Shakespearean Theatre of Maine, a.k.a. the Theatre at Monmouth. All summer its actors, including Goldie, weave magical renditions of classical and even some newish dramas. And each summer, for a handful of performances, the theatre's cast concocts an enchanting matinee offering for children (and bears) of all ilks. You have a good chance of finding Maria, Nicholas, Carrie and the rest of the clan ... especially Goldie. If, by chance, they're having tea, stick around. You're bound to find magic.

Tiny Teddies

MATERIALS AND SUPPLIES

- ■ 1/8 yard (.11 m) woven-backed mohair fabric. A good pile length is 1/4" (.6 cm)
- ■ 4" (10 cm) square of paw pad fabric
- ■ Two 5 mm or 6 mm glass teddy bear eyes or onyx beads*
- ■ Sewing thread to match mohair fabric
- ■ Fine-line permanent marker
- ■ Small, sharp scissors
- ■ 6 joint discs of diameter 1/2" (1.3 cm) and 1/16" (.15 cm) thickness. Four joint discs of diameter 3/4" (1.9 cm) and 1/16" (.15 cm) thickness
- ■ 10 very thin and pliable cotter pins, 1" (2.5 cm) long
- ■ Polyester fiberfill
- ■ Mini-bear stuffing pellets (optional)
- ■ Perle cotton or embroidery floss
- ■ Needle-nose pliers
- ■ Stuffing stick with fine tip
- ■ Dental floss or strong (upholstery) thread for inserting eyes
- ■ Sewing machine or hand-sewing needles and thimble
- ■ Embroidery needles
- ■ White glue and toothpick
- ■ Seam sealant (optional)
- ■ Awl

If this bear is intended for a child, please embroider the eyes with black perle cotton or embroidery floss.

There's something magical about a bear you can hide in a pocket. A bear just fitting the cradling palm of one's hand or into a dollhouse or (time for confessions!) the prayer book rack at church, is ... well, near-perfect. He can be a confidant, a companion, a secret conspirator and travel partner. Or a bear for your bears to love. These 5½" (14 cm) tall "pocket bears" are fully jointed and made of rather shortish mohair. A funny thing happened when they got sewn up. Although they were done using exactly the same patterns and techniques, the two pastel-colored bears grew. Their mohair (which was regular, not sparse) had a stretchy backing. In every direction, they're a little larger. "Bear" this in mind with all the patterns in this book. The fabric you use has its own personality, so all sizes here, as in every project, are approximate.

I'll bet you can't make just one of these guys. They're a delightful addiction. You can get at least a couple of bears from ½ yard of fabric. Save the scraps for a "patchwork" little guy. In this size, you get a bunch of bears for minimal mohair, saving you almost enough to purchase the bifocals you'll need once you discover you can't make just one.

Maria and tiny Maria.

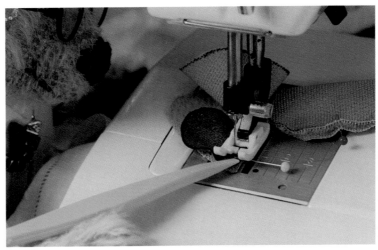

Photo 1

Photo 2

INSTRUCTIONS

Construction is done with right sides of fabric facing and seam allowances of 1/8" (.3 cm), unless otherwise noted. See Tips and Techniques section of book for guidance in pattern preparation, cutting, sewing, and jointing. Please see Project 5 for general directions on making a fully jointed center-seamed head bear, but follow jointing directions below.

The instructions below are tips on making tiny teddies. They do not cover each step, but are the extra things to "bear" in mind.

1 Before sewing by machine, pin pieces together and hand-baste in thread the color of fabric, which won't be removed. Pieces of fabric this small (especially mohair) slip around if not basted before machining.

2 Sew with 1/8" (.3 cm) seam allowances. A left-needle setting, if your machine has it, gives more control. Use small stitches. Sew seams twice, using matching thread, over basting.

3 These bears are a good size to sew by hand, but machine-sewn seams are stronger. Sewing these little pieces can be tricky, however. Sometimes it's good to grab onto the piece with a tool (an orange stick or shishkebob stick is good) as it is passing under the sewing foot (Photo 1).

4 A Teflon™-coated foot helps sew difficult surfaces, especially the synthetic suede or garment-weight leather many use for paw pads. Paw and foot pads like those pictured (for little Maria bear), made of garment leather, are stretchy and difficult to sew. Make the

extra stitching on the foot pad, to secure while turning right-side out (see Photo 2).

5 After limbs are stitched, snip seam allowances with embroidery scissors on curves of legs and arms before turning right-side out and stuffing.

6 Use needle-nose pliers to turn limbs right-side out after sewing.

Photo 3

Photo 4

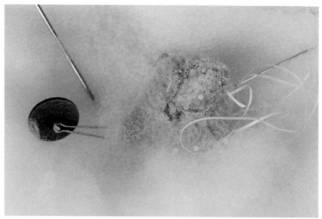

Photo 5

7 Jointing little guys is like jointing big ones, only more delicate. All the jointing materials fit the scale of the bear. Jointing discs and cotter pins are thinner. Discs have tinier holes, so little cotter pins won't pull through. When sewing arms and legs, do not leave tops open for stuffing. Sew right around the whole seam line. Use the slit method (see section on Jointing in Tips and Techniques). This eliminates the hand-sewn seam at the outside limb top you would have otherwise. On tiny bears, it's difficult to sew these closing seams neatly. If you use the slit technique, closing seams at the joints are hidden. Slits are length of joint disc diameter plus 1/4" (.6 cm) or the amount of give you need to insert the disc and/or turn the limb (Photo 2). Slide the disc into limb (this is done the same way on arms). Slit is just large enough to accommodate disc with a

tad wiggle room. Photo 3 shows what the legs look like when using the slit method of disc insertion. The slit on the leg at left looks sorta raggedy. This disappears when sewn up, as on the leg at right in Photo 3. Note: this leg contains a wobble joint made with 2 cotter pins. The head of the inner cotter pin protrudes to the leg exterior. Cotter pin joints in bears this size can be rolled into snail joints. Grab one end of cotter pin with tip of needle-nose pliers and roll it into a coil around tip. (See Jointing section of book for details.)

8 Photo 4 shows how and where to place jointing discs to determine where to put joints. To attach limbs, make a dot with marker through hole in disc onto mohair to mark limb placement. The cotter pin from bear's head in Photo 4 points at the little slit you've marked and clipped at body top.

9 Tiny teddies feel especially nice if mostly filled with plastic pellets. Teddy bear specialist suppliers sell an especially tiny-scale stuffing pellet. These little "beans" scatter everywhere if not corraled. Maria stores her pellets in a plastic container. To fill smallish body pieces, she takes the top off a small candy container with a hole in the top, scoops up pellets, replaces the lid, directs the lid opening over area to be filled and pours pellets into it. Stuff body pieces softly, so they'll move and scrunch nicely.

10 Heads in these smallish bears feel nicely scrunchy if partially stuffed with pellets. Photo 5 shows how tiny these items are. Just plop the body part onto the bed of stuffing as you work.

Photo 6

Photo 7

Photo 8

Photo 9

11 Top off pellets with a bit of fiberfill so they won't pop out of part. Note: the head joint in Photo 6 is a floppy or wobble joint, made with two cotter pins. See Project 5 for basic instructions on closing and embroidering the head. When you insert cotter pin from bear's head into body through slit, inside body, add jointing disc on cotter pin and roll cotter pin ends into snail joint with needle-nose pliers to secure (Photo 7).

12 When you embroider claws onto arms and legs, make arm claws nice and long, please (Photo 8).

13 Attach arms to bear at marked spots by poking cotter pins through fabric at holes and finishing joints inside body with disc and snail joint, as you did for the head. Attach legs to bear at marked spots in the same manner (Photo 9). You will have an empty, jointed bear.

14 To stuff hump and crotch areas of body with fiberfill, use stuffing stick.

15 Fill body loosely with pellets, then top with fiberfill at back seam. Close stuffing opening slowly, with ladder stitch (see Closing Seams section of Tips for details), molding body with your hand, inserting bits of fiberfill or pellets if needed to make it feel good when scrunched.

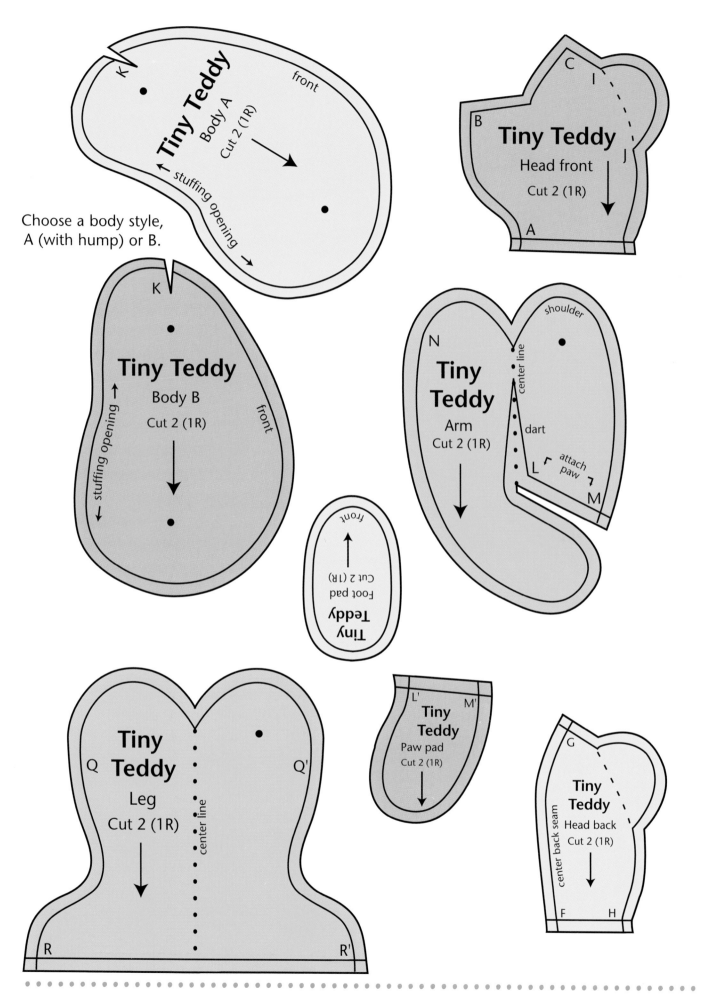

Tiny Teddy
Body A
Cut 2 (1R)
front
stuffing opening
K

Choose a body style,
A (with hump) or B.

Tiny Teddy
Body B
Cut 2 (1R)
front
stuffing opening
K

Tiny Teddy
Head front
Cut 2 (1R)
C I J
B
A

Tiny Teddy
Arm
Cut 2 (1R)
shoulder
center line
dart
attach paw
N
L
M

Tiny Teddy
Foot pad
Cut 2 (1R)
front

Tiny Teddy
Leg
Cut 2 (1R)
center line
Q Q'
R R'

Tiny Teddy
Paw pad
Cut 2 (1R)
L' M'

Tiny Teddy
Head back
Cut 2 (1R)
center back seam
G
F H

SECTION I:
Fabrics Through Stitching

FABRICS

Mohair for Bear's Body

The bears in this book will best come to life if they are made from mohair fabric. This hard-wearing, luxurious fabric, made from angora goat fleece woven onto a stable cotton backing, is traditional teddy bear fabric. One encounter with a bear made from mohair will tell you why. It just feels like the real thing.

Types of Mohair. Most of the mohair available to the home sewer is loomed in mills in England or Germany. Each country's product has distinct peculiarities. Their backings differ. When you buy mohair, pay attention to its backing. If it's too stiff, or too loose, your bear may not turn well, or it may fray. Either way, it will be no fun to sew. English mohair seems a bit scruffier than German. This can be a plus if it fits your bear's personality. German mohair, at this writing, offers an ever-expanding supply of finishes and colors; English mohairs offer their own distinct versions.

Pile. Mohair pile (the fleece woven into the backing) comes in lengths from approximately $1/8$" (.3 cm) to over 1" (2.5 cm) and finishes ranging from straight to wavy, ultra-dense to ultra-sparse (indicating how many strands of mohair are woven into the backing), and in a wide variety of colors.

Finishes, lengths and backings used give each type of mohair a particular feel. The best way to acquaint yourself is to contact a specialist fabric importer and ask for samples of its English and German mohairs. When you receive them you will discover some have stiffer or looser woven backings, some are bristly, some are soft; some feel just right. Choose mohair with flexible but not loosely woven backing so it will turn nicely, but not unravel in cutting and sewing.

A $1/2$" (1.3 cm) mohair pile looks different if sparsely woven, distressed, curled, or feather-finished. The bears in this book are made from sparse mohair, with fewer strands of mohair than normal woven into backing. This gives them an

old-fashioned, soft, broken-in-already feeling. I have made them in various mohairs and with a lovely woven-back synthetic fabric. They all came out charming, but their personalities changed with each experiment.

Photo 1

Photo 1 is a closeup of four types of sparse mohair: distressed, curly, feather finished, and straight. Notice how easily you see through to the backing. Photo 2 shows a wider variety of mohair fabric finishes and colors. Most of these mohairs are sparse. I like the way it handles and the way it feels when made into a bear. I also like the way sparse mohair cuts, and that there is less fur to get caught in the seams, or to pick out of them when sewing's done.

Mohair is expensive. As with any project you undertake, the better materials you use, the nicer your bear will turn out. Think of mohair for your bear as an investment ... in a lifelong friend.

Photo 2

Synthetic Fabrics

If you can't get your hands on mohair, you can still use these patterns. The firms in Germany weaving mohair yard goods also produce high-quality synthetic plush with woven backings. They keep to grain and are some of the most luxurious, softly huggable fabrics imaginable.

Fabrics for Paw and Foot Pads

The part of a bear a person is going to handle most is the paw. It should be strong, appealing, and feel good. It is nice to use a paw pad fabric with the same weight and hand as the body's fabric. This is why I use cotton velveteen for paw and foot pads. It's strong and sensuous. There's nothing quite so lovely as holding onto a soft velveteen paw pad. I'm talking about woven-backed cotton velveteen, the kind sold around Christmas-time for luxurious party dresses—not velvet. Velvet smooshes around when you cut it out. The little velvet fibers tend to fall out in time, and feel, I think, a bit peculiar. If you want to experiment, here are paw pad choices other than velveteen, some new, some traditional.

The first row in Photo 3 features good quality wool felt. Most early bears were made with wool felt paw pads (usually these pads were underlined with another layer of felt). Don't confuse this felt with the shabby synthetic stuff you find in crafts stores. Wool felt is sturdy, easy to use, keeps it shape and feels nice and ... well, secure ... to the touch when made into a paw pad.

The problem with felt is it's just not durable enough — not for an active bear. Take a look sometime at the holes in the paws of antique bears. If you are intending to spend a lot of time with your bear, you want his paws to hold up to the adventures you'll be planning. Felt is traditional, but methinks it's time for new traditions and experiments. However: It's good to keep a small stash of felt on hand in nose-shade colors, because it's the best stuff around from which to build up the base for a nice, substantial bear nose.

The second row in Photo 3 shows the color range available in synthetic leather and suede. This lovely, pricey fabric is strong, resilient, and feels good to the touch. It is easy to cut and comes in a veritable rainbow. Its one drawback: It's a bit tricky to sew on. The face of synthetic suede tends to stick to the presser foot. But this can be gotten around by using a Teflon™ foot on your sewing machine.

Photo 3

This slick, coated foot slides nicely over conflicting paw pad and body fabric surfaces and textures.

As it has no nap, no grain, and doesn't fray, synthetic suede is as easy and economical to use (in terms of layout, not price) as felt. Lay it out to best utilize the fabric. One can pin synthetic suede (as opposed to real suede and leather). It will recover from pinholes, if you use fine pins and immediately sew up the fabric. But don't leave pins in overnight; holes left this long may take a long time to close.

Synthetic suede is nifty to keep on hand to make personalized sewn-in labels for bears (Photo 4). I usually write bear's name, mine, and any other pertinent information in indelible ink on such a label, and sew it into the bear's rear seam.

In the third row of Photo 3 are samples of garment-weight leather and suede. Choose paw pad leather with a good hand. It has to bend and respond to movement in the same way as the fabric you use for your bear's body. If it does not, you're in for frustration. The paw pads will probably look as if they don't want to be on that bear.

Photo 4

THREADS

Construction Threads

You need a number of different specialized threads to create your bear. Most are available at yard goods stores. Buy the best quality thread. You will find the bear construction business easier if your thread is strong, flows easily through your sewing machine, and does not shed fibers all over your machine's bobbin case.

Any good-quality sewing thread should, hypothetically, work, as long as you match it to the color of your bear's fur. I prefer cotton thread to polyester thread. This is usually available as quilting thread, although it doesn't come in as many colors as regular thread. It's strong, but not fancy. It's not too heavy. It's suitable for sewing all but the tiniest of bears. If you can't get cotton thread, a poly-cotton blend works.

I've used other types of thread, including invisible thread, which I use in the machine to sew miniatures like little Maria bear, 2½" (1.3 cm) tall. I sometimes use upholstery thread to sew bear openings closed and sometimes to attach eyes. I also use dental floss for this purpose. You might want to keep some beeswax with your supplies; it is useful for hand-sewing. Run hand-sewing thread through beeswax to discourage knots and tangles.

The sturdy threads in Photo 5 can all be used to sew bears' eyes securely into their heads. They are (clockwise from upper left): sturdy bead-stringing thread, sinew bought at a jewelry-making shop, upholstery thread, and dental floss. Not pictured, but also useful, is monofilament fishing line. It's very strong, comes in many weights, and is available at your local sporting goods shop.

Photo 5

Embroidery Threads

Perle cotton (*coton perlé*) is the traditional thread used to embroider bears' faces and claws. It comes in a number of weights. You'll probably use size 3 and size 5, available in skeins of many hues, for regular-sized bearmaking projects (Photo 6).

For smaller bears, you might want to experiment with finer widths of perle cotton; the higher the number, the finer the thread. A visit to an embroidery shop opens a world of possibilities to the tiny-bear maker. You might choose traditional 8-strand skeined embroidery floss, or try some lustrous silk thread, my favorite choice for a luxurious mini-bear's schnozz.

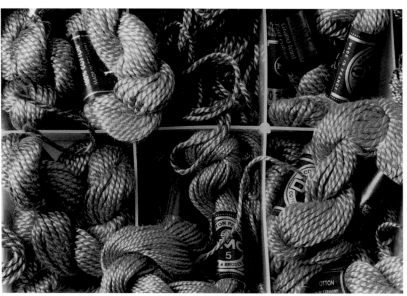

Photo 6

EYES

Please note: the eyes I describe below are intended only for teddies made as collectibles or for adults. If you make the bears in this book for children, you must use plastic safety eyes, modifying construction techniques to do so. Better yet, embroider them, using black perle cotton.

The bears in this book all have shoe-button eyes or glass eyes that look like shoe buttons. They are all black, all pupil. I've never used anything else. Why? I think such eyes have more soul. Psychologists say the amount of the black part of the eye visible when a person looks at you indicates the way he feels about you. The more black, the more affection. I think a bear should convey a message of complete love, hence the shoe-button eyes. The first teddies had them. Why mess with tradition?

Photo 7

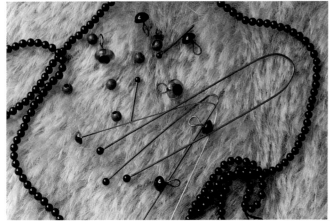

Photo 8

Photo 9

Photo 10

Shoe buttons can be found. Check bear or doll-maker magazines or Web sites. Shoe buttons come in a variety of sizes and finishes: usually black or brown, shiny or matte, some, even, with little white pupils in them, from around 7 mm to 11 mm in width, the latter suitable, perhaps, for a 12" (30.5 cm) bear (Photo 7). If you want a shoe-button effect for a larger bear, you'll need to investigate blown glass eyes that are all black.

Glass eyes can be had in a variety of styles and qualities. Eyes are hand-blown; size of the eyes, and of the pupils in them, varies. Be careful in matching a pair to put into your bear, lest he look strange. Better quality eyes tend to be more consistent in size and shape.

Glass eyes usually come with a metal loop on back, or attached to a metal rod, with one eye on each end. To use the latter, cut the rod in the middle, bend a bit of the metal rod into a loop with needle-nose pliers, and cut off the excess.

For smaller bears, a visit to a jewelry-making shop or a fishing supply shop should turn up any number of possibilities. Photo 8 shows a strand of onyx beads, which make lovely eyes in small bears, and eyes on rods, as well as the matte black bead items shown, intended as eyes in fishing lures. To store your bear's eyes and other bearmaking odd bits, sort them by type into clear 35 mm film canisters, which fit perfectly into the boxes sold in craft supply shops for storing embroidery floss. One glance tells you what's in the box.

JOINT DISCS AND COTTER PINS

Although there are various ways one might joint teddy bears, I still prefer the old-fashioned way: joints made with cotter pins and discs. This is the method used for many projects in this book. It is flexible, easy-to-do, and materials used are commonly available. The joints I use are extra loose and flexible, so the bears have extra opportunity to come to life. The head and limbs are prepared as separate units and can rotate on the cotter pins and discs that connect them to the body. The cloth of the limbs and head is not stitched to the body for this kind of joint. Important: If you are making the bears in this book for a child, use plastic safety joints instead.

For lack of alternatives, I used metal fender washers for joint discs like the one pictured at bottom center in Photo 9 in Yetta, the first teddy I designed. These proved durable but weighty. Most bearmakers today use hardboard joints, available in many sizes and styles. Bearmakers today are fortunate to be able to buy joints, and cotter pins to go with them, to put together even miniature teddies.

Cotter pins, straight from the hardware shop, work fine to joint bears. They come in all sizes and in various metals, from brass to steel (Photo 10). Make sure yours will easily bend; some, like the one directly under the large brass pin in Photo 10, are far too thick and brittle to make nice joints.

FILLINGS

I've always felt a teddy's most important job is solacing object, to be always ready and approachable. To achieve this, I filled the bears in this book with a mixture of high-quality polyester fiberfill and plastic pellets. Good polyester fiberfill has long fibers. When you shake it, little if any falls away. It packs well and resists shifting. Traditional old teddies were filled with excelsior (wood shavings). Some used kapok or lamb's wool. Except for miniature bears, in which I use cotton, I like loosely stuffed fiberfill and plastic pellets in limbs, well-packed fiberfill in the head, and a nice mixture of fiberfill and pellets in the body, making sure there's a nice, scrunchy

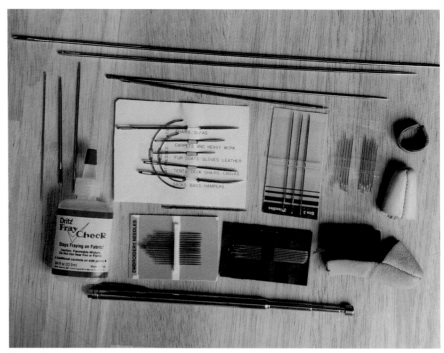

Photo 12

bunch of pellets in the tummy area. If I had a source of soft lamb's wool, though, I might replace the poly-ester fiberfill with lamb's wool for my personal teddies because it's "real" and feels good. The fill-ings shown in Photo 11 include cotton, plastic doll pellets, and several styles of fiberfill. Important: If bear is for a child, don't use pellets or any flamma-ble fillings. Use polyester fiberfill instead.

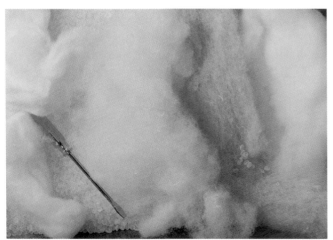

Photo 11

BEARMAKING TOOLS

Sewing Machine and Needles

Unless you plan to make bears by hand, you need a sewing machine. A straight stitch machine will do. A zigzag one is better. One with a choice of stitches and feet for sewing a variety of fabrics is even better. See the section on Stitching Your Bears for

specialized feet that help with stitching and for further tips.

Mohair fabric is heavy and sturdy. Use a sewing machine needle strong enough to sew denim (a jeans needle is perfect). If one's not available, choose at least a size 14 needle with a sharp tip, not a ballpoint. Change the needle often, and start each project with a new one. A dulled needle caus-es frustration and messy stitching. If you're sewing synthetic plush with a knitted back, use a ballpoint needle, same sizes as above.

Hand-Sewing Needles and Accessories

Even if you stitch the bear together by machine, you will need some specialized hand-sewing nee-dles. Some may be new to you. The long needles at the top in Photo 12 are dollmaking needles, some-times known as upholsterer's needles or toymaker's needles. Use these to attach eyes to the bear's head. Other useful needles are embroidery needles and, of course, regular sewing needles. My favorite needle for bearmaking is one intended for leather work. It has a chiseled point on the end, which comes in handy when making noses or sewing up body parts. I've only found it in sets of all-around utility needles. Match needle to task at hand: use fine needles for tiny bears.

Change the needles often. You'll need a thimble to push the needle through without hurting your hands. The three unusual thimbles in Photo 12, two leather thimbles and one quilter's thimble, protect fingers from bearmakers' punctures.

Use seam sealant to prevent raveling when you puncture fabric to make joints or insert eyes. The gizmo at the bottom of Photo 12 is a telescoping wand. The size of a pen, it has a magnet on one end. Extended to full length, it can pick up pins or other metallic doodads dropped to the floor.

Pliers and Stuffers

Needle-nose pliers in a variety of shapes and sizes are useful for making crown joints for bears. For some projects you'll need 2 pair. Very pointy ones are good for jointing very small bears. Stuffing sticks in a variety of shapes are available from sewing shops, bearmaking specialists, supermarkets, and hardware stores. The one with the round handle in Photo 13 is a favorite: made from a screw driver with a wooden ball glued to the top, it is comfortable and accurate to use. Not pictured: everybody's favorite stuffing stick: the chopstick, available at your local Chinese take-out.

Photo 13

Cutting Implements and Cleanup

Get a couple pair of good, sharp shears. You'll need a largeish size for cutting out mohair, and a pair of embroidery scissors for trimming work. Find scissors to fit your hands and working methods. I enjoy the new, ergonomic scissors shown in Photo 14. They come in large and medium sizes, make cutting much less arduous, and save hands. Also pictured: 2 types of bent-nosed shears, lovely for cutting and embroidery work, and a pair of small locking forceps, good for stuffing small items and for turning small limbs and pieces right-side out. The white-handled stiletto in Photo 14 is an awl, used for making holes in fabrics. Also shown is a rotary cutter, and a pen-sized knife, invaluable for cutting all sorts of stuff.

Photo 14

My favorite scissors swirl around the center on a chain (they're called chatelaine scissors). I wear them around my neck like a necklace when sewing and feel like an elegant Victorian needlewoman.

Also useful for cutting: A single-sided industrial razor blade. This type blade has a handle to grab on one side. Use the razor blade to cut through backing of single layer of fabric. With practice, one can cut plush, especially synthetic knitted-backed plush, quickly using a razor blade. A mat knife works, too. Use a cutting mat underneath to protect your table.

For cleanup, keep a vacuum cleaner handy to control the fuzz and fluff. Best plan: vacuum each piece as you cut it out. This removes fallout at the source. Another method of fluff control: Chuck cut-out pieces into your clothes dryer, on the air setting. The excess fluff will collect in your dryer's filter. It's far better to collect it there than on your clothes, your floor and everywhere you carry your in-progress bear.

Styling Brushes

When your bear's born, you'll want to brush his fur into a fitting coiffure. The brushes pictured in Photo 15 help. The large one, sold at pet stores for grooming (as well as pet combs) desnarls and untangles the stubbornest mohair locks. The little finger brush, sold by bear parts suppliers and embroidery specialists, does the same thing. Be careful! Its teeth are like needles.

Photo 15

PATTERN-MAKING SUPPLIES AND TIPS

Transparent plastic in flexible rolls, sold in a variety of thicknesses at drafting supply and art stores, is good for creating permanent pattern templates. To use, place it over the pattern pieces in the book and trace, using a permanent marker. Then cut them out of the flexible plastic. As an alternative, you might photocopy the patterns, glue them to cardboard, and then cover them with adhesive-backed clear plastic, sold to cover books or shelves. The plastic will make patterns more permanent. To label the pieces, use a permanent marker that can write on plastic.

WORKING WITH BEARMAKING FABRICS

Finding the Straight Grain of Fabric and Laying Out Pieces

Each pattern piece in this book has an arrow showing how to align it on the straight grain of fabric. In bearmaking there are two considerations:

1. As in regular sewing, align arrow with the warp or weft threads, the straight lines of weaving in the fabric. (For pile fabrics they're seen on the back of the fabric.)

2. Consider the direction the pile is to go when cutting the pieces. You want all the pattern pieces to have the pile going in the same direction—top down—arms, legs, body, and head. If you cut against the grain (on the bias, say) for some of the pieces, they will not behave the way the rest of the pieces do. Your bear may not fit together properly, or sew or stuff well. You want your bear to be sturdy and well-done; please resist the temptation to scrimp on fabric by laying out pieces at strange angles. Run your hand along the fabric. It should feel smooth when you run it with the nap down. If you look carefully, the pile should fall downward. I say "should," because sometimes it doesn't. Mohair mills are coming out with lots of new, nifty finishes. Some, especially the distressed sort, look so swirly and scrambly it's hard to tell which way is up. Some change and backtrack direction in the middle. If you are befuddled, take a deep breath, choose the way you think most of the pile goes, and cut the bear along the straight grain of the backing in that direction.

3. Many pattern pieces have a mirror image or reverse that you need to cut. For example, the right side of the head is the mirror image of the left side of the head. This is indicated on the pattern piece as: "Cut 2 (1R)," where R stands for "reverse." In that case, trace one of the pattern onto the fabric; turn the pattern over, and trace the reversed pattern once also. For jointed bears, holes for limb attachment should only be marked on the inner side of the arm or leg (the side that will face the body).

4. Changing nap direction. If, once the bear is made, you don't like the way the fur lies in a section, you can change its direction. Wet the pile. Do not soak it; this is a styling session, not a bath. Brush it the way you want it to go. After styling, let it dry. If it's stubborn, you might use a hand-steamer along with a bear brush (one with wire bristles, bought at a pet shop) for styling. Mohair is a natural fiber, so it can be set like hair. Yep, you can even use mousse and hair spray, if you are desperate to style your bear's coiffure. Your bear will then smell like a beauty parlor. He may not like this.

Photo 16

Photo 17

Working with Knitted-Back Synthetic Plush Fabrics

Warning: Knitted-back synthetic plush will stretch. This will alter the shape of the finished bear. The fabric is created with the pile knitted into it. It will stretch in at least one way, sometimes both. You must prevent the back from stretching before drawing your pattern pieces onto the fabric or your bear will look Most Peculiar. Here are two handy ways:

1. Attach a lightweight interfacing or stabilizer to the back of each piece. Test your fabric first to see what happens to it if you iron on an interfacing. You may have to stitch the interfacing to the seams of each piece before sewing (just outside the seam allowance stitching line), instead of ironing. The backing not only keeps the plush from stretching, it can also help prevent the edges from fraying. A lightweight nonwoven Pellon® interfacing is a good choice. Make sure it's flexible. No stiffness allowed here! Tricot-backed interfacing is newish and flexible. It doesn't add much weight to the plush, but adds control.

2. If you don't use interfacing, cut out the pattern pieces in lightweight muslin as well as plush. Pin the muslin to the back of the plush layer and sew the two together as one. Pay attention to the grain, keeping the fabrics aligned on the grain line when cutting out.

CUTTING BEARS OUT

Important: See section above on finding the straight grain before starting to cut. Here are some tips for cutting mohair and other bearmaking fabrics:

Photo 18

1. You want to cut the backing of your fabric, not the pile. Lay out pattern pieces with the back of the fabric facing up, and position them so the pile runs down the body parts.

2. Choose a pair of smallish to medium shears that feel good in your hand (the new, ergonomic scissors are ideal) or a razor blade. Small scissors give much more control than larger ones. Use a snipping motion and cut plush through a single thickness, through backing only, leaving the pile undisturbed. For fast, mess-free cutting, use a razor blade, carefully. Carefully cut along lines you've drawn on the back of bear's fabric. This method of cutting may take a tad longer, but you will be rewarded with luxurious, long pile on your pieces, and very little pile fallout.

PREPARING PIECES FOR STITCHING

Because the fabric you will be using to make bear has pile, you need to do a bit of seam allowance preparation before sewing.

1. Trim fur in the seam allowance down to the fabric backing, to make stitching easier, and seams less bulky (Photo 16).

2. Even if you use very short-pile mohair, fur on seam allowances should be clipped so edges fit nicely together and don't fight when you stitch.

3. Hairdresser's thinning shears work well to clip fur on areas like muzzles (Photo 17). Always clip these, especially in the seam allowance, before sewing pieces together. You can do fine-tuning of the area after bear's head is stuffed. Ergonomic scissors make clipping less tiring.

4. Take your time when clipping fur in places like the nose area of the head gusset. Remove a little fur at a time (Photo 18).

5. Clipping doesn't need to be even at this stage. You just want to prevent lumps and long fibers in seam allowances, especially in face area.

STITCHING YOUR BEARS

Although it is possible to hand-sew bears, I suggest you use a sewing machine; your seams will be stronger and more uniform. Almost any machine will do. A zigzag stitch is a plus for finishing edges. If you are blessed with a sewing machine with bells and whistles, you can put them to use making bears. Here are a few tips on using your machine to advantage in bearmaking, plus some other helpful hints:

1. Mohair's sometimes a slippery critter to stitch, as are some of the materials used for paw pads, like synthetic suede and leather. I've found two specialized sewing feet, available for many sewing machine models, helpful in tackling both mohair creep, that annoying tendency of one layer of your mohair seam to slip away while stitching, and the feeding problems one encounters while stitching difficult fabrics. The cute little item in Photo 19 is called a Teflon™ foot. It's a plastic foot that is coated so it chugs along over rather difficult fabrics. Here, it's sewing mohair. You'll note that, in this book, photos show the use of this foot or the big one in the next shot. The frightening contraption in Photo 20 is actually a good friend to sewers of mohair or any other fabrics which tend to slip. It is called an even-feed or dual-feed foot. While pricey, it eliminates much of the slippage inherent in sewing mohair. If you sew a lot of bears, it might be worth investigating.

2. You probably have a favorite way to judge sewing seam width. I prefer the sewing of a 1/4" (.6 cm) wide seam with the even-feed foot, using markings engraved on the machine's metal plate to judge seam width. My machine has variable settings for needle positions. In Photo 21, the needle is set in the left position, which I prefer. I feel it gives more control over stitching. To sew a 1/4" seam in this position, I align the outer toe of the foot with the edge of the fabric.

3. Reduce presser foot pressure, loosen thread tension. Test your stitches on scraps to find the best settings.

4. When you pin seams, push pile towards the inside of the body part before sewing, so it doesn't catch in seam.

Photo 19

Photo 20

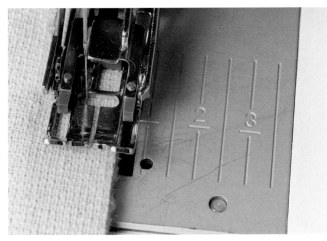

Photo 21

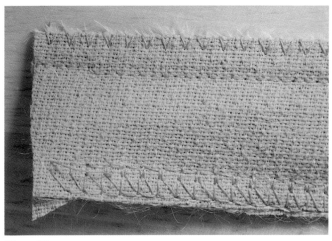

Photo 22

Photo 23

Photo 24

5. At top of Photo 22, you see the traditional seam treatment for bearmaking: a straight stitch at the seam line, and a zigzag stitch at the edge (2W, 3.5 L) to prevent fraying. At bottom in the photo is a built-in stitch that sews the seam and finishes the edge in one step. There are a variety of stitches and seam treatments useful in sewing bears. Any stitch or combination that will sew a sturdy seam and overcast the edge is fine.

6. Sometimes, when you are sewing areas with a lot of curves like ears or the muzzles of bears, you don't want to overcast the edges of all the seams. Photo 23 shows the combination of seam treatments I use. By now you've noticed my seaming is hardly glamorous (all right; it's sometimes downright gnarly). Don't worry if yours is a tad wobbly. Nobody will know but you and the bear.

7. When you come to a tricky area like the one where the curve of the head gusset meets a straight part, give the front of the gusset a tug until the seam pulls straight, instead of being sort of notched. You can sew a straight seam all the way down to the gusset's front this way. The gusset will just bounce back into place.

8. Sometimes you need a little help guiding mohair around tight curves in areas like foot pads, especially if the fabric has long pile. Look in your kitchen drawer for a chopstick, an orange stick for pushing cuticles, a shiskebob stick, or dowel to grab fabric and push it into place (Photo 24). Sure beats risking fingers!

9. When you're done sewing curves, notch them by clipping the fabric in the seam allowance, before trying to turn the bear parts right-side out. This is especially important on places like ears, where curves can be dramatic. Be sure to avoid cutting into the seam line, of course (Photo 25).

STITCHING FOOT PADS

Setting in foot pads on your bears should be easy if you follow the following tips:

1. Fold foot pad in half, along long axis from front to back. Put a pin into the crease at each end. The leg pieces should be stitched together and wrong side out. Insert a pin at center front and center back of leg, at foot opening. With right sides of fabric together, match front of foot pad to front of foot, at pins. Pin together (Photo 26).

2. Pin foot pad to foot bottom, in seam allowances, easing to fit (Photo 27).

3. Using straight stitch, sew pad to foot, stitching all around until you reach your start, and backstitching at start and end, removing pins as you sew. Work with the pad side facing you (Photo 28).

Photo 25

Photo 26

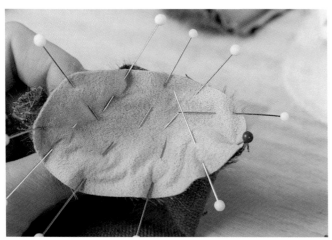

Photo 27

Photo 28

MAKING JOINTS WITH DISCS AND COTTER PINS

When I contemplated making my first bear, the scariest and most mystical part of the procedure was joints. I use the time-honored disc-and-cotter pin jointing method. (However, if you are making a bear for a child, use plastic safety joints instead, as explained later in this section.) The function of the joint is to let the arm, leg, or head rotate. There is a disc or large washer in the limb or head and another disc in the body of the bear; they are connected by one or two cotter pins. The limbs and head are sewn closed so the only thing holding them to the body is the cotter pin, and they can rotate well.

To hold the cotter pin and disc together, it is necessary to spread out the ends of the cotter pin. That is the function of the snail or crown joint, which curves the ends of the cotter pin and snugs them up to the disc. We'll explain exactly how to do this in the parts that follow.

Photo 1 shows the various types and sizes of basic cotter pin joint components: a cotter pin (or two), a small washer (or two), a couple of discs or large fender washers, and a pair of needle-nose pliers, chosen to complement the size of the joint you're making.

Photo 1

Note: the tops of the cotter pins pictured vary. I prefer the pin at top right (Photo 1), with the big funny-shaped top. It doesn't pop through the joint's hole when you're bending the cotter pin. Choose pins that bend readily, or you'll soon get sore, tired fingers. For comparison, see Photo 2. This cotter pin has a tiny head. It will pull through the hole in the disc when cotter pin is bent in joining. To prevent this, slip a little washer onto the end of the pin first, before adding the disc.

Photo 2

Crown Joints

We are about to make a crown joint unit using two discs, two cotter pins, two washers, and needle-nose pliers. Most joints used in this book are done in this way, and are wobbly or floppy, which lets the limbs move around freely. Photo 3 shows components.

To make a floppy joint, you will need to bend two cotter pins: one before inserting joint into limb and one after the limb is closed, while you join limb to body. I'll go into this later. But first let's learn how to make a crown joint:

1. Thread a tiny washer onto a cotter pin (to keep the cotter pin from pulling through the disc). Thread cotter pin through disc.

Photo 3

Photo 4

Photo 5

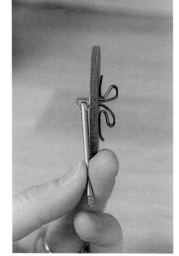

Photo 6

Photo 7

2. Use pliers to bend ends of cotter pin into a wide "V" shape (Photo 4).

Photo 8

3. Bend one widened end of pin back onto itself, using the pliers' nose (Photo 5).

4. Using pliers, grab the section of cotter pin between hole and the bend just made. Pull it down, back, and under the curve. The part of cotter pin bent backward towards hole in Step 3 now lies flat against disc and points outward towards disc perimeter (Photo 6).

5. Repeat this process on other side of the widened pin. Make sure pin ends lie flat against disc (Photo 7). To make a floppy joint unit, a crown joint like the one made above has a second cotter

pin inserted in the head (round end) of the first cotter pin as in Photo 8. Then the unbent cotter pin is threaded through the body and a second disc is added to the cotter pin. After that, a second crown joint is made to secure the disc inside the body.

Diagram 1 shows a comparison of a double cotter pin (floppy or wobbly) joint and a single cotter pin joint.

Diagram 1. Crown joints made with (left) single cotter pin and (right) double cotter pin. Wobbly joints are made with double cotter pins.

Photo 9

Photo 10

Snail Joint

If a crown joint is too daunting, you can simply roll the ends of your cotter pin into a spiral on either side of the hole, to make a snail joint (Photo 9). This technique doesn't put as much tension on the joint. I don't think it's quite as strong. It's especially useful for joints in very small bears, or when you just can't get crown joints to behave, however. Photo 10 shows wobble-joint units held with snail joints, ready for insertion into a smallish bear. On smallish bears the snail joints have more than adequate strength.

Order of Jointing, Stuffing, and Assembling

The order of things is usually as follows:

1. Stuff head and insert disc joint unit in neck. Stitch closed the head opening around the protruding cotter pin. Embroider face. Clip head attachment slit at top of body; then attach stuffed and jointed head to unstuffed body, securing it with a second disc and crown joint inside body. Note: If you are using plastic safety eyes instead of embroidering eyes, they must be inserted into the head before it is stuffed.

2. Make attachment hole on body side (the side facing the body) of each arm or leg. Partially stuff each limb, leaving room for disc joint mechanism. Insert joint disc unit in limb with cotter pin protruding through attachment hole to outside of limb.

3. Finish stuffing limb and stitch it closed around cotter pin.

4. Insert limb's cotter pin into correct limb attachment hole in body and attach the limb inside body by adding another disc, a washer, and bending the cotter pin to secure it. Do this for all 4 limbs.

5. Stuff the body and stitch it closed with ladder stitching.

We'll explain all this in more detail in the coming sections.

Marking Limbs for Disc Location and Attaching Them

1. To figure out where to locate joints on limbs, choose a disc slightly smaller than upper part of limb (hip or shoulder). Center disc on limb, on the side of the arm or leg that will face the body. Pull it down a bit from edge — the limb's size determines how much. Larger limbs require more space at top (Photo 11).

2. Poke nose of a permanent marker through joint hole in disc, making mark on fabric where attachment hole should be.

3. Use awl or tip of embroidery scissors to make hole in one layer of limb fabric at this point. Try to make hole between fibers, so you don't fray fabric. This isn't possible on large limbs. Apply seam sealant to hole to keep from raveling. Allow to dry.

4. Turn limb right-side out, find hole, and make a location reference dot on furry side of limb with marker.

Photo 11

Photo 12

Photo 14

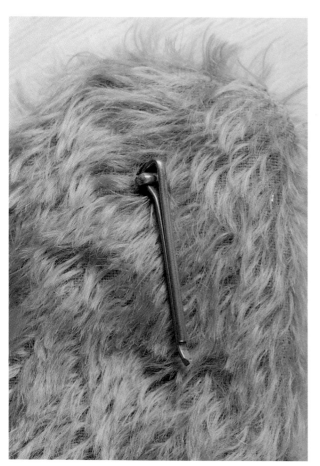

Photo 13

5. Prepare joint for insertion into limb.

6. Insert disc joint unit in limb and poke cotter pin from the joint through attachment hole in limb's fabric. Enlarge hole with scissors if necessary (Photo 12).

7. For a wobbly cotter pin joint, head of inner cotter pin must push through hole in limb to the outside of the limb's fabric. Thread a second cotter pin through the protruding head of the first cotter pin (Photo 13). Push the second cotter pin through the correct hole in the bear's body, from outside to inside. On the inside of the as yet unstuffed body, add a disc (and a washer, if desired), and make a crown joint or other joint to hold it (Photo 14).

Photo 15

Photo 16

Joints for Smallish Bears

Use thinnish joint discs, $^1/16''$ (.15 cm) thick, sold by bearmaking suppliers. Use thinnish, very pliable cotter pins. Use needle-nose pliers with tiny tips. Coil each end of cotter pin around nose of pliers to make a snail joint. The rest of joint can be done as for larger bears, but see Slit-Limb Method below.

Jointing Option: Slit-Limb Method

This method is especially good for smallish bears. It eliminates sewing up seams on outer limb edges.

1. After marking joint insertion hole in limb, cut a slit the length of the diameter of joint, half above and half below joint insertion hole (Photo 15). Prepare joints for insertion into limbs. Turn limbs right-side out, using stuffing implement.

2. Stuff limb firmly in foot area, softly in the rest of leg. Leave unstuffed space to insert joint.

3. Insert joint unit into leg, making sure the rounded end of the cotter pin inside limb sticks out through the slit. For wobble joint, attach a second cotter pin (Photo 16).

4. Sew up slit in limb with thread that matches limb.

5. Attach limbs to body as for larger joints. When bear is jointed, no one will see the slits. Commercial manufacturers use this method for big bears, too. Why not try it?

PLASTIC SAFETY JOINTS

Plastic safety joints should be used in bears made for children. Once the plastic safety joint mechanism is locked together, it can't come apart, so no little parts can fall off and be eaten. A plastic safety joint consists of a disc with a built-in pin, a plastic washer, and a second disc that locks onto the pin. To use, insert the joint disc with the pin into the inside of the arm or leg, and poke the pin out through the prepared hole in the arm or leg fabric, as you would with a cotter pin disc joint. Push the pin through the correct hole in the bear's body fabric, add the plastic washer to the pin inside the body, and secure the joint with the locking disc. Push the locking disc onto the pin as far as possible.

STUFFING TIPS

When stuffing your bear, always remember that the bear's innards should be as fine as the outside. Use high-quality stuff. It will not only be easier for you to use, but it will make your bear feel and wear better. Old-timey bears were stuffed with wood

wool, or excelsior (think of the curlicues of wood you see in wood shops). Actually, excelsior comes in grades, and there's one still made specially for teddy bears. Check out teddy bear specialist vendors, especially anyone in Germany, for a lead. However,

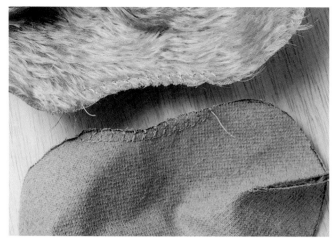
Photo 17

Photo 18

don't use excelsior for any children's bears, as it's highly flammable. Choose a nonflammable stuffing instead.

I like my bears soft and responsive. I use high-quality polyester fiberfill and a couple of different sizes of plastic pellets to fill them. If I had a source for sheep's wool, I might consider using that in part, since I like the idea of natural innards.

Consult the order Jointing, Stuffing, and Assembling (p. 112) in the jointing section to know when to stuff the various parts. The idea, when stuffing a bear, is to make him look all of a piece, with no lumps or peculiar areas. Here's how I do it.

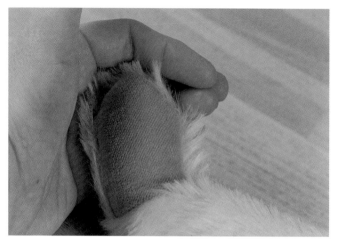
Photo 18A

1. After you cut out your limb and body pieces, machine overcast raw edges of the pieces where the stuffing openings will be (see patterns) with zigzag or other stitch (Photo 17). Assemble each limb and the head as directed in project.

2. Fluff out a handful of polyester filling. Roll it onto the tip of your stuffing implement. Insert stuffing by little bits, starting at the most difficult to fill areas. In head, this would be the nose. Make sure it's nicely filled and rounded before going on to the rest of the head. Stuff around the perimeter of the area. Then fill in the middle, using the same amount of pressure everywhere.

3. Wrap stuffing bits around stuffing tool (Photo 18). Cradle body part you're stuffing in your hand as you fill it with fiberfill, making sure it keeps its shape (Photo 18A).

4. Round and shape the body part with your hand all the time you are stuffing, so no lumps or hard spots develop, and to control flexibility in the limbs.

Photo 19

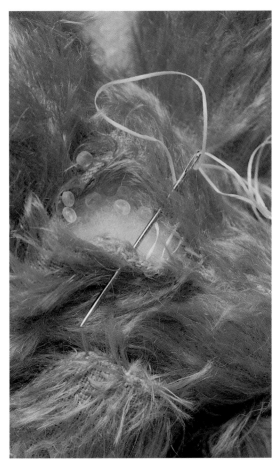

Photo 20

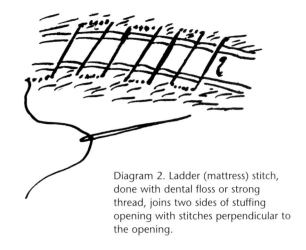

Diagram 2. Ladder (mattress) stitch, done with dental floss or strong thread, joins two sides of stuffing opening with stitches perpendicular to the opening.

5. Pour stuffing pellets into a box or basin big enough to hold the largest body piece you will be stuffing. Fill a small container such as a film canister with pellets. Pour pellets into body part little by little, taking time to pick up part from time to time and see how stuffing's coming along (Photo 19).

6. After you've filled a part with pellets, and before you sew it closed, add a bit more fiberfill to cushion edges and to help keep pellets inside.

7. It's a good idea to sew up anything you've stuffed with pellets right atop that pellet container to avoid spills. Pellets have a fiendish tendency to bounce everywhere.

CLOSING SEAMS

The ladder stitch (or mattress stitch) is easy to do and closes seams almost invisibly. Choose a sturdy thread (upholstery thread, or dental floss are good) and a sturdy needle. Work from right-side of fabric through only one thickness. Don't turn seam allowances under before stitching; they will turn to inside as you pull stitches tight.

Knot one end of thread. Enter fabric from wrong side, hiding knot. Come out on seam line, then insert needle into the seam allowance on the other side of the opening that's directly opposite the side of seam you started on. The crossing stitch is perpendicular to the seam allowance. Take a small stitch in the fabric, $3/16''$ (.45 cm) or less, parallel to the seam line and come up on the same side of the opening. With needle and stitch parallel to first stitch, make a stitch into first side. Take another small stitch under the seam line. Continue taking stitches from one side to other, keeping stitches parallel (Photo 20 and Diagram 2). Every couple of stitches, pull thread tight. Your stitches will disappear. When your seam is done, knot thread. Point your needle from beside the knot through the stuffing and out through the fabric, pull thread, and clip, losing its tail in the bear.

HINTS FOR HEALTHY BEARMAKING

Bearmaking, like any craft, can become a passion, even a lifestyle. I hope you derive a lifetime of pleasure pursuing it. One way to keep bearmaking a pleasure is to pursue it safely. As with any craft or art, there are hazards in making bears. If you know what they are before you begin, you can avoid them. The good news is: today's sewing market has all sorts of gizmos to help keep your bearmaking healthy. Here are a few I use.

1. Protective masks. You will soon discover, once you start making bears, that your immediate world is covered with fluff, chiefly mohair or synthetic plush fibers. If you decide to make lots of bears, I recommend you invest in protective masks — the kind painters wear is fine — to cover your nose and mouth so you don't breathe in the fibers (Photo 21).

2. Covered drink canister or tea cup. I couldn't consider making bears or anything else without a good cup or a glass of tea. I found a Russian tea glass holder in an antique shop in Arkhangelsk, Northern Russia. It's covered with a ceramic cover when not in service. This keeps mohair from flying into the brew. A travel mug with a cover on it is a good choice.

3. Footrest. I use a footrest when sewing (Photo 22). It's big enough to fit not only the foot pedal of sewing machine, but my left foot, so both feet get elevated at the same angle. I can tilt and vary its angle as I sew, so my legs aren't stuck in the same position, my feet don't fall asleep, and they feel as if they belong to me. Specialist sewing catalogs offer footrests designed for this purpose.

4. Slanted board. My sewing machine is sitting on a clear plastic slant, specially manufactured for sewing machines. It brings the machine, and the work on it, to the user's line of sight. It's designed to help prevent strain from bending over to see what you're working on. A couple of versions of this item are available. Works for me. But it is pricey. You can get the same effect if you elevate the back of your machine with a couple of square artists' erasers or a pair of slanted rubber door stops.

5. Under my machine, I've a flannel pad. It not only keeps the machine and the plastic slant from scratching the table, but lessens any movement or noise the machine might make. When it gets filled with thread and mohair, I toss it into the wash.

6. Timer. One of the biggest complaints of people who make a lot of bears is carpal tunnel syndrome: a tingling and numbing in the fingers and wrists, which can, if not treated, severely limit their use. This condition comes from doing motions over and over, using the little muscles and tendons of your hands and wrists. Typists, computer operators, and people who assemble parts in factories develop carpal tunnel syndrome. You won't, if you work safely.

   Limit the amount of time you do any particular bearmaking procedure, especially if you make a bunch of bears at once. It is far healthier, though less time-efficient, to make each bear from start to finish than to do the same step ten times in a row. The muscles in your arms and hands were not made to withstand the repetitive, abusive motion involved in stuffing the parts of

Photo 21

ten teddy bears in one fell swoop. Every hour or so, get up, stretch, move around. Set a timer, if you lose track of time, so you'll know when to take a break. If you take care of your body and learn good working habits from the start, your bearmaking experience will be not only happy, but healthy.

Photo 22

SECTION III:
Making Faces

Maria poses for a closeup.

The nose on a bear is truly the signature of its designer, as much as a brush stroke is a signature of a painter. Here are options for making noses for the bears in this book. I hope you will experiment and figure out a nose that is yours alone. Don't worry about perfection. A little IMperfection adds character. You can always take stitches out and try again. Cut out nose-type shapes from flexible paper (used laundry fabric softener sheets are good for this). Try paper noses on the bear before putting thread to schnozz area. When you come up with a keeper use it as a guide. The embroidery needle I frequently use has a wedged point. It is made for sewing leather. I prefer this needle for embroidering noses. It cuts through stuffing and layers of fabric.

Nicholas in his red nightcap.

Nicholas, in a pensive moment.

FEATURES FOR CENTER-BEARS

Drawing the Nose Freestyle (Maria and Nicholas)

This is my favorite way to make a nose; I feel I'm drawing the nose with embroidery thread.

1. Clip nose-embroidery area of bear's face so it's even and nearly free of fur pile (Photo 1). This can be done before pieces are assembled. Hair-thinning scissors can be used, or regular scissors.

2. With pins, indicate bear's mouth location (and eyes, if you've not yet sewn them in). Pins should be in a sort of triangle: one pin, a bit down from the bottom of the nose, shows where to sew the line attaching the nose to the mouth. The other two pins show the halfway mark of bear's smile. Thread perle cotton or embroidery thread of your choice into a large needle. Take a stitch at the side of the face, no knot attached, to temporarily anchor thread. As soon as you begin stitching the nose, you can cut this end away. Insert needle into one side of nose. Poke needle through nose and come out at same level on other nose side. Make a straight stitch across front of nose, to get an idea where the middle line of the nose will be (Photo 2).

3. Determine where you want nose's top and bottom. Insert a pin in nose, at head-center seam.

4. Loop perle cotton over pin atop the nose. Take a stitch, bringing needle out at bear's left side of nose, where it started (Photo 3). You have defined your nose's top.

5. Repeat this procedure at the bottom nose half. At this point, the vertical pin holds the two parts of the nose perimeter in place.

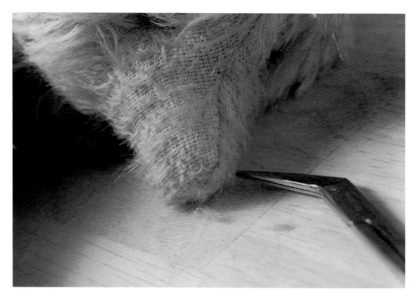

Photo 1

Photo 2

Photo 3

6. Begin to fill in the middle of the nose, taking a stitch first on top, then on bottom, of center stitch. After a few stitches, anchor both top and bottom of nose, where the pin holds them, with little stay stitches (Photo 4). I wait a few stitches before I do this. The nose wants to take on its own shape. It's good to give it a chance before committing to a final choice.

7. Continue filling in nose with satin stitches, taking one stitch above and one stitch below the ones you've worked until nose-middle is filled.

8. Make outline stitches around nose perimeter: four of them. From the left-hand corner, sew a stitch to the center top and a stitch to the center bottom. From right-hand corner, sew a stitch to the center top and a stitch to center bottom (Photo 5).

Mouth and Eyebrows for Freestyle Nose

1. Let's finish bear's face. From the bottom middle part of nose, make a stitch straight down to the middle pin below it. Make an inverted "V" below that stitch, by sewing down to the pin on the bear's left, then up to the center again. Repeat stitches on the right (Photo 6). Bring needle out at bottom of stitch on the left-hand side, at pin.

Photo 4

Photo 5

Photo 6

Photo 7

Photo 8

Photo 9

Photo 10

2. Complete the up part of bear's smile with a stitch. If you are unsure where you want it to end, play around with pins until the effect pleases (Photo 7). Usually this is at the same level as bottom of nose. Then pass needle through head under nose to point chosen on bear's left-hand side. Bring it out, and complete left side of the smile's top.

3. Make a stitch at a 45 degree angle to the smile and insert needle gently under mouth's corner, to catch stitch into a smile line. Push needle through snout, coming up at same level on the other side. Stitch downwards, this time, to

complete the smile, bringing needle out in from and below eye (Photo 8).

4. For making eyebrows, at a 45 degree angle to the center seam, insert needle behind and just above bear's right eye. Take a stitch to other side of face as shown (Photo 9). Make another angled stitch for second eyebrow. Do these stitches once more, to define and draw eyebrows.

5. Insert point of strong needle (or awl) into head, to smoosh the stuffing around, sculpting face-contours to your liking (Photo 10).

Photo 11

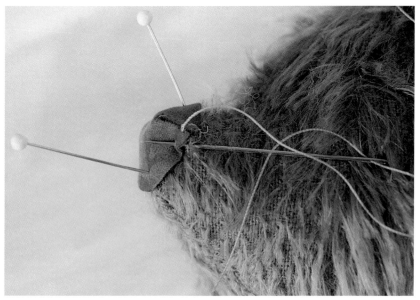

Photo 12

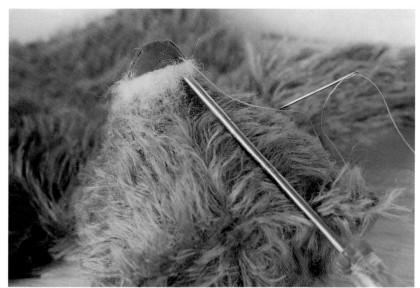

Photo 13

Template-Type Nose

1. If you want an exact and dupli-catable area onto which to embroider your bear's nose, consider using a template. Photo 11 shows the shape template I use on Maria and Nicholas. I make it out of paper, fit it onto the nose, then cut it out of felt to match nose's thread color. Experiment with template shapes to create the nose shapes you want. After cutting out template from felt or whatever, sew up the V-shaped darts, using a very small seam allowance.

2. Fit nose template onto bear and pin. Tack-stitch to either side of snout (Photo 12).

3. Sew bottom of nose template to snout with more little tacking stitches, leaving top open. The tacking stitches won't show later on.

4. If desired, add a bit of stuffing to nose from top with a pointed tool (Photo 13). This makes a rather schnozzy nose, as you'll see.

5. Finish stitching the nose tem-plate to bear snout (Photo 14).

6. Embroider over the template as for the freehand nose described above, vertically or horizontally (Photo 15). It will take a lot of embroidery cotton to cover a well-stuffed nose.

Embroidering a nose vertically can be seen in Photo 16. Note how prominent the stuffed-template nose is.

Finish face embroidery as de-scribed under Mouth and Eyebrows for Freestyle Nose, above.

Photo 14

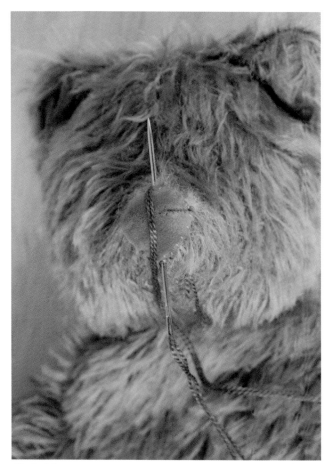

Photo 15

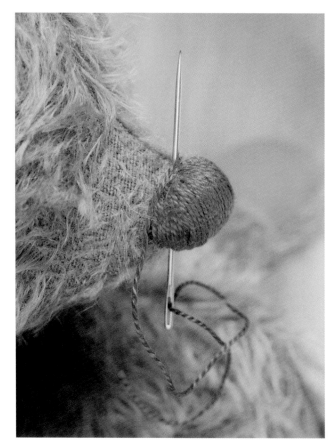

Photo 16

Photo 17

Photo 18

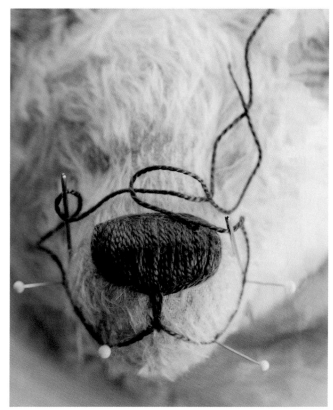

Photo 19

1. Trim fur on gusset's nose area if you haven't already done so.

2. Cut a pattern for the shape of nose you want, trace the shape onto felt, and cut out. Note: The illustrations show 2 shapes of noses.

3. Pin felt where you want bear's nose. To ensure even stitching, try inserting long needles along nose's edges and using their hard edges as a sewing template (Photo 17). Satin stitch, horizontally or vertically. This nose has vertical stitches. I find short vertical stitches easier to control. Take one stitch at a time on either side of the center nose stitches.

4. When satin stitching is done, frame the nose with outline stitches as for freehand nose (Photo 18).

FEATURES FOR GUSSET HEAD BEARS

Using Felt Nose Templates for Heads with Gussets

This method is useful if bear's head has a gusset and you want to control the nose's shape while sewing it, as well as give it a bit of heft. I used it for Professor Ted and Carrie.

Face Embroidery with Gusset Noses

1. Mark shape of bear's mouth with pins. If you want bear to smile, mark point at which smile will turn up, and where it will end. Thread two identical long needles with the same perle cotton. Sew a central stitch vertically between nose and mouth with each needle and thread. Then drape thread underneath pins from middle to back of the mouth. Insert each needle vertically at end of the smile (Photo 19) and bring out the points of each

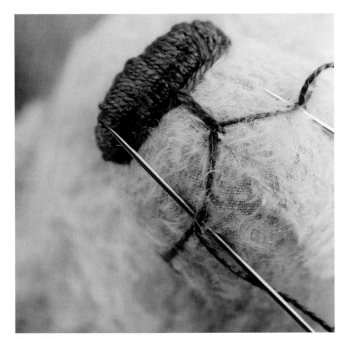

Photo 20

Photo 21

Photo 22

Photo 23

needle where bear's smile bends to make a stitch. Take tacking stitches on each side to hold draped threads (Photo 20). Make sure everything is even on each side. Bring needle out at smile corner of each mouth-half and make mouth corner stitch at an angle to end of mouth.

2. Proceed as for Nicholas and Maria for eyebrows (Step 3 and 4).

3. The completed nose and mouth on Carrie and Professor Ted can be seen in Photo 21.

4. If you're making a smaller bear, like this 12" (30.5 cm) Ted, you might choose to embroider the rest of his features with techniques used for Maria and Nicholas (Photo 22).

5. Here's Professor Ted with the smallish version of him. Both have vertical stitching on noses, but their shapes are slightly different. Ted's personality shines through, no matter how his face is stitched (Photo 23).

Björn Teddy Bear Family Album

Professor Theodore Roosevelt (T.R.) Björn: Teaches arctology at Teddy Bear University, atop BlueBeary Hill, in the State of Maine.

Carrie-Lynn Bearke-White Björn: Wife of Professor Ted; a world-famous photojournalist and fashion designer who teaches photojournalism and fashion design at Teddy Bear University. Carrie and Professor Ted have three children: the twins, Maria and Nicholas, and their older sister, Jenny-Lynn.

Nicholas Carl Jonathan Björn: Twin brother and traveling companion of Maria. Nicholas enjoys tea, traveling, books, computers, and religious inquiry.

Maria Alma Oskara Björn: Enjoys tea, traveling, sewing and needlework, exploring, and the theatre.

Jenny-Lynn Björn: Older sister of Nicholas and Maria. Jenny-Lynn is a graduate of the New York Fashion Institute, where she studied fashion design and traditional embroidery techniques. She has been making quite a reputation with her heirloom sewing and intricate embroideries, some of which adorn the altar and vestments at St. Mark's Church.

Edward Bearian: Jenny-Lynn's fiancé. Originally from New Jersey, Edward met Jenny-Lynn one summer in New York City while pursuing his dream of becoming a master chef at the New York Cordon Bear Internationale. After graduation, Edward moved to Maine and opened, with Jenny-Lynn, the Black Bear Tea Shoppe, Bakery and Stitchery Emporium.

Rosalind Golden, a.k.a Goldie, Star of Stage and Screen. A porcelain doll, born on Staten Island in New York City, who became one of the world's most versatile and beloved actresses. As a child, she sat for Carrie as a photographic model. The publicity photos Carrie took of her launched Goldie's acting career. They became fast friends, and when Carrie moved to Maine, Goldie followed her.

BluBear Yu and Rosa BonneBear: BluBear Yu is also known as BlåBjörn (BluBear). Mascot of Teddy Bear University. A legendary figure, BluBear Yu and his wife, Rosa BonneBear, founded Teddy Bear University as a ladies' seminary in the early 19th century.

The Rev. Dr. Carl Oskar Björn, D. D.: Professor Ted's father; has been rector of St. Mark's Church, BlueBeary Hill, Maine, for over 30 years. He has a wry sense of humor, and he loves to knit.

Anastasia Nikolaevna Björn: Carl Oskar's wife. Born in Arkhangelsk, Russia. They met at a concert in Sigtuna, Sweden, one summer while he was on student holiday. He fell in love with her at first sight. Both knew they would never again meet, were Anastasia to return to Russia, so they married at once.

INDEX